THE
Self-
Esteem
WORKBOOK

THE SELF-ESTEEM WORKBOOK

Inspired by *You've Got This!* by Poppy O'Neill (published 2021). Text by Caroline Roope.

An Hachette UK Company
www.hachette.co.uk

Vie Books, an imprint of Summersdale Publishers Ltd
Part of Octopus Publishing Group Limited
Carmelite House
50 Victoria Embankment
LONDON
EC4Y 0DZ
UK

www.summersdale.com

Printed and bound in China

ISBN: 978-1-80007-716-4

Substantial discounts on bulk quantities of Summersdale books are available to corporations, professional associations and other organizations. For details contact general enquiries. Telephone: +44 (0) 1243 771107 or email: enquiries@summersdale.com.

THE
Self-
Esteem
WORKBOOK

Practical Tips and Guided Exercises
to Help You Boost Your Self-Esteem

ANNA BARNES

Contents

Disclaimer

This book is not intended as a substitute for the medical advice of a doctor or physician. If you are experiencing problems with your health, it is always best to follow the advice of a medical professional. If you have any health issues, consult your doctor before undertaking any new forms of exercise.

Introduction

Welcome to *The Self-Esteem Workbook*, a handy guide for learning to accept and love yourself – flaws and all. When we have good self-esteem, we're able to enjoy life to the full, taking pleasure in the world around us, tackling the tricky stuff with confidence and seeking out new opportunities. Yet sometimes, for lots of different reasons, we become uncomfortable in our own skin. Even the most self-assured among us experience periods of uncertainty – it's part of being human. Most of the time, these feelings don't last long and we're able to carry on living a happy, healthy life, but, occasionally, negative thoughts can start to affect our self-worth, leaving us unhappy and frustrated.

The good news is that there are many ways to boost your self-esteem. This means the next time a challenge presents itself, you'll be ready to tackle it with a positive outlook and a renewed sense of self-worth.

Taking those initial steps on a journey of self-discovery can often be the hardest, but they're also the steps that lead to the most noticeable, positive change. So bravo for being pro-active – you've got this! Using a mix of ideas, activities and techniques employed by therapists, such as cognitive behavioural therapy (CBT) and mindfulness, you'll learn how to recognize the signs of low self-esteem, explore how to make positive changes and nurture a healthy relationship with yourself. After all, it's the most important and long-standing relationship you'll ever have.

I was once afraid of people saying, "Who does she think she is?" Now I have the courage to say, "This is who I am."

Oprah Winfrey

What this book will do for you

This book will enable you to understand the importance of self-esteem and its effect on your well-being. You'll learn how to boost your self-belief, gain the confidence to be true to yourself, and recognize your strengths and positive attributes – even when times are tough.

Self-esteem is one of the key factors in living a happy and fulfilled life. It pushes us to succeed, allows us to achieve new things and helps us overcome obstacles. When we believe in ourselves, we can make better decisions and be resilient when life doesn't go to plan. The more you learn about yourself, the easier you'll find it to believe that you *do* matter and you *are* good enough. It's a bit like un-learning what you *think* you know about yourself. So, if you're ready to stop listening to negative self-talk and eager to make a positive change, you've come to the right place.

How to use this book

This book is for you if...

- **You tend to focus on your flaws.**
- **You're sensitive to criticism or negative feedback.**
- **You put your achievements down to "luck" rather than hard work.**
- **You compare yourself unfavorably to other people.**
- **You've convinced yourself you're a "bad person" or no one likes you.**
- **You feel like you're not good enough.**
- **You feel like you need to be perfect constantly.**
- **You tolerate bad treatment from those around you.**

If this sounds like you sometimes (or all the time), this book is here to help. You can learn to love yourself, but doing so takes conscious action – only you have the power to change your relationship with yourself for the better.

These pages provide a blend of holistic advice, practical exercises and useful tips which will assist you to build your self-esteem. While there are lots of techniques on offer, what suits each person will vary. You are the best judge of your own needs. The most important thing is to progress at a comfortable pace that feels right for you.

Remember, you already have all the tools and potential inside you to boost your self-esteem – but may need a little nudge in the right direction, coupled with some self-belief. So read on and get ready to discover a new you!

PART 1

Self-esteem and you

Enhancing self-esteem should be simple, right? We get promoted at work, we start a new relationship with someone exciting, or we pass an exam at college. But if it's so simple to increase our self-esteem, why do so many of us have low self-esteem some – or even all – of the time? If this thought resonates with you, then you've picked up the right book!

The best place to start your journey to greater self-esteem is by looking at the relationship you have with yourself. After all, the knowledge that it's OK to be you lies at the heart of a healthy self-esteem, and if you truly believe that you are great exactly as you are, your confidence and self-esteem will blossom. Sometimes, though, it's hard to be objective about yourself, particularly if you give too much headspace to critical self-talk. However, becoming comfortable with who you are and what you're all about is the first step on the road to healthy self-esteem. In this section, we'll be exploring what self-esteem is, what causes low self-esteem and how we can work towards a more balanced view of ourselves.

Making sense of yourself

WHEN YOU KNOW YOURSELF,
YOU ARE EMPOWERED.
WHEN YOU ACCEPT YOURSELF,
YOU ARE INVINCIBLE.

Tina Lifford

How many of us *really* know and accept who we are? It's so easy to lose sight of ourselves as we go through life, especially if our responsibilities change, bringing with them a host of personality-eroding duties and obligations. And if that wasn't frustrating enough, we often fall into the trap of trying to live up to the unrealistic expectations of social media, in a world that sends us constant messages about who we *should* be and what we *should* be like. It's little wonder we lose sight of that special something that makes us... well, *us*!

But all is not lost. While it can sometimes be a lifelong project figuring out who you are, what you value and what's important to you, it's never too late to start that journey of self-discovery. And finding your authentic self is integral to nurturing healthy self-esteem, because it means you'll have the strength of mind to cope with setbacks, make decisions that are in your best interests and approach life with a positive mindset.

A helpful way to get started on the road to self-discovery is to interview yourself. Jot down some answers to the prompts below, making sure each answer is a true reflection of how you feel, rather than what you think you *should* feel.

Which three words best describe me?

When and where am I the happiest version of myself?

What are my greatest attributes?

What are my biggest weaknesses?

How do I measure success?

What would I like to be remembered for?

What am I afraid of?

What single piece of advice would I give a younger version of myself?

What single piece of advice would I give my future self?

I can't live without...

So, what is self-esteem?

Self-esteem

Self-esteem is the way we value and perceive ourselves. It's based on the opinions and beliefs we hold about ourselves – the tone of which can be either negative or positive, depending on how healthy our self-esteem is. It does not mean thinking you are the best at everything – rather, it's being comfortable with who you are, even when life doesn't go to plan. It means accepting yourself, with all your strengths and weaknesses, and having confidence in your own abilities. Put simply, it's about trusting and having faith in yourself.

Self-esteem exists on a scale – it can be high, low or somewhere in the middle, and the things that affect it differ for everyone. It's also true that your self-esteem can fluctuate throughout your life – for instance, because of a sudden major life event, such as the breakdown of a relationship or loss of a job. Or you might have had low self-esteem for a while – even as a young person – which could make it harder for you to identify and address it.

But know this – you're not alone. Statistics collated by London-based psychotherapists, Harley Therapy, state that up to 85 per cent of the world's population are thought to be affected by low self-esteem – that's a lot of people undervaluing themselves! But you can change your experience by taking it one step at a time.

What does high self-esteem look like?

Taking pride in your achievements

Being able to make decisions and assert yourself

Having the confidence to try new and difficult things

Taking time out for self-care

Being kind to yourself, physically and mentally

Moving on when things go wrong without blaming yourself

Believing you matter and are good enough

Liking and valuing yourself as a person

Knowing you are valued

Recognizing and celebrating your strengths

Understanding your weaknesses

Feeling comfortable in your own company

What does low self-esteem look like?

Negative thinking

Ignoring or discounting strengths, talents and positive qualities

Focusing on flaws, weaknesses and mistakes

Blaming yourself when something goes wrong

Finding it difficult to move on when you make a mistake

Being overly self-critical

Feeling worthless and questioning why people like/love you

Not taking care of yourself, physically and mentally

Spending time with people who don't have your best interests at heart

Comparing yourself unfavourably to others

Worrying about what other people think of you

Being easily influenced/going along with the crowd

Worrying about how you look and act

Looking for reassurances from others

The self-esteem quiz

Take this quiz to get an idea of how high or low your self-esteem is right now. Circle the answer that sounds most like you...

1. I believe I'm good at...

a. Plenty of things

b. Nothing at all really

c. One or two things

2. When I compare myself to others, I feel like...

a. I'm a good person and so are they

b. I'm definitely worse than them

c. I'm better than them

3. To me, perfection is...

a. Not a real thing!

b. A necessity, or I won't be liked

c. Something I never quite achieve, but I can just about live with that

4. If I make a mistake, I...

a. Try to put it right, learn from it and move on

b. Look for someone else to blame and refuse to let it go

c. Feel awful, but put it right, chalk it up to experience and move on

5. My friends...

a. Are fun, kind and great to be around

b. Frequently put me down, but at least they talk to me

c. Are OK – I'm closer to some than others

6. When I do well...

a. I feel proud of myself and want to share it with others
b. I think I should have done better and am annoyed at myself
c. I feel embarrassed to talk about it, but will share my success if I'm encouraged

7. Saying "no" is...

a. Sometimes tricky, but I will assert myself if I feel my needs are more important
b. Unkind. What if people decide they don't like me as a result?
c. Something I try to avoid, but I do assert myself occasionally

Mostly As: you have high self-esteem and a healthy amount of self-belief. You understand the importance of self-respect, and you know how to value yourself and others. This book will help you to strengthen it even more, as well as recognize the signs of low self-esteem in others.

Mostly Bs: your self-esteem is low. You tend to put yourself last and you worry about what other people think of you – even if they treat you disrespectfully. You need to spend time cultivating a healthier opinion of yourself and recognizing your worth. Your feelings matter – don't ignore them!

Mostly Cs: you could do with working on your self-esteem, so you can maintain healthy self-belief on a daily basis. You know how to give yourself a boost when you're feeling down, which is great. Strengthening your self-esteem will help you feel good about yourself, whatever happens.

Checking in with yourself

It's so easy to forget about our own needs, particularly if one of our roles is to provide care for a loved one that requires us to focus our attention on them. But even without that responsibility, we often live our daily lives outside of ourselves. We engage in conversations with others at work, at home and on social channels. We're bombarded with the drama, news and opinions of others via the media. Our mental space is almost always occupied by external forces. But how much of your day is spent in conversation with yourself?

An essential part of nurturing your emotional wellbeing involves spending time with yourself. And guess what? Inviting yourself into your "inner world" not only keeps you balanced – the self-knowledge gained is important for boosting your self-esteem.

So, grab ten minutes of quiet time and ask yourself how you're doing. Try not to get distracted. To focus your attention, write down how you're feeling. Concentrate on thoughts, emotions, physical sensations – whatever comes to mind. In this safe space, you're free to assess your physical and emotional needs.

What does high self-esteem look like to me?

The concept of self-esteem and how it develops has been keeping psychologists busy for decades. What makes things trickier is that humans are a complicated species and everyone is a unique individual – so what looks and feels like low or high self-esteem to one person may look and feel different to the next.

Deciphering how you think you might feel and act if your self-esteem was healthier is a useful tool for encouraging you to visualize yourself in a positive light. It also provides a target to work towards that's based on your own beliefs about how high self-esteem would influence your life, rather than what's expected of you by others. Use the space below to jot down some ideas. There are some prompts if you need them!

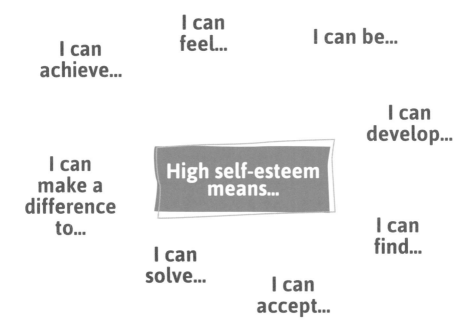

What influences self-esteem?

We all carry with us a unique set of experiences that can influence our self-esteem. As we journey through life, it can sometimes feel as though we're negotiating a range of mountains, complete with peaks, troughs – and several heart-stopping precipices, too! No wonder the challenges sometimes feel endless. While these can alter over time, any one of these obstacles can knock our self-esteem off course, particularly if we're already feeling vulnerable. Here are some of the most common influences on our self-esteem:

- **Upbringing**
- **Friendships**
- **Relationships**
- **Past experiences**
- **Traumatic events (past and/or present)**
- **Work**
- **Health**
- **Social circumstances**
- **Achievements**
- **Social media**

But as you know, it isn't all doom and gloom – the lows you experience are simply part of the rich fabric of life, and learning to handle these with resilience can help to boost a healthier sense of self-esteem. While we can't always control what happens to us, we can control how we choose to feel about it and, with improved self-esteem, you'll gain the mindset needed to deal with mistakes and failures in a more positive way.

How does low self-esteem affect us?

Having low self-esteem can make all areas of our lives difficult. In relationships, you may feel insecure and find it hard to trust other people. You could also find it hard to set boundaries, which can leave you vulnerable to manipulation and coercion. You might avoid challenging but rewarding opportunities, such as going for a promotion or learning a new skill, because your fear of failure prevents you from trying. Over time, poor self-esteem can slowly chip away at your emotional well-being, leading to low moods, anxiety and depression.

If this sounds familiar, you're certainly not alone. A study conducted in 2020 by the Body Shop on the self-esteem of 22,000 people across 21 countries found that one in two people worldwide felt more self-doubt than self-love, while around 60 per cent wished they had more respect for themselves. Below are some examples of the types of statements people with low self-esteem might make:

I don't feel confident expressing a different opinion in front of my friends.

I didn't apply for the job because I didn't think I would be good enough.

I stayed with a partner who put me down and was unfaithful to me.

I used to love painting, but I'd get really upset if I made a mistake, so I don't bother any more.

I stopped going to the gym, because everyone else looks better in their gym kit than me.

On social media, other people's lives appear to be more fulfilling than mine, so I had to start faking photos to keep up.

How can you work towards high self-esteem?

Learn to like yourself! That's the simple answer, but the reality can be somewhat trickier.

You might not have considered this before, but the way you think and feel about yourself often just seems like "the truth", and you assume that's how everyone else thinks about you, too. But to develop better self-esteem, you need to challenge this notion by looking at alternative possibilities, carefully considering your thoughts and actions, and asking questions. Only then will you be able to change the way you see yourself.

However, there is no instant fix. If we want to develop a healthy self-esteem that can withstand all the ups and downs that life throws at us, it will take a little time and patience. Sure, there are ways to get a quick self-esteem boost (such as posting a selfie of your new haircut online to get "likes", or donating to charity), as well as situations that knock your self-esteem temporarily (like tripping over in public or failing a test), but the aim is to come back to roughly the same healthy level, once you've moved on from these boosts and knocks.

Restoring your sense of self-worth will not solve all your problems, but it will help you find courage you never knew you had, as well as renewed faith in your own resilience to bounce back from failure. You absolutely can do this!

PART 2

Self-esteem boosters

Having a healthy self-esteem is possible for everyone. We all deserve to feel good about ourselves, value our existence and take pride in the things we're able to achieve – whether it's running 3 km for the first time without stopping or developing a successful multi-national business. What matters is how you feel about yourself inside.

Over the next few pages, you'll find tips and gentle activities to help you explore your thoughts and emotions. Being attuned to how you're *really* feeling will help you to improve the relationship you have with yourself, which is crucial for building healthy self-esteem. Listening to what your mind is telling you through the noise of everyday life takes practice, but it's worth persevering. It's a bit like finding the clearest signal on an old radio – you just need to keep turning your inner dial until your own voice comes through loud and clear.

These activities are designed to help you take that first step out of your comfort zone, break patterns of negative thinking and create new experiences. So, whether you just need a little nudge, or a full-on boost to crank up the noise, get ready to say hello to yourself!

Meet yourself with meditation

Meditation is a wonderful introduction to your mind and emotions. If you haven't tried it before, it can feel a bit strange to start with, but the more you do it, the easier it becomes. Meditation can help to change the relationship you have with your thoughts, which is a vital part of building self-esteem and increasing your confidence.

You can meditate anywhere, but a comfortable chair in a quiet room is a good place to try it out. If you live with other people, ask them not to distract you. Here's how to start:

- Set a timer for three minutes, or choose a relaxing song to listen to (when you get to the end of the tune, you'll know you can finish meditating).

- Sit comfortably and close your eyes.

- Think about your breathing: how each inhale feels, followed by each exhale. Don't hold your breath in between – just try to breathe slowly in through your nose, then out through your mouth. Listen to the sound of your breath.

- Imagine your mind is a clear, blue sky. If any negative thoughts start to intrude, think of them as clouds simply floating by that will pass, leaving the sky blue again.

- When the timer goes, or the music ends, open your eyes slowly.

And here's the science behind it...

A happy mind is calm, clear and positive. But when we burden it with negative thoughts, it can get cloudy, dark and even a bit stormy, making it easier for low self-esteem to take hold. Meditation is a powerful tool, because we learn that no matter how cloudy the sky becomes with negative thinking, there will always be a calm, blue sky on the other side. Meditation helps us to recognize those thoughts as just "passing." Instead of identifying with them or using them to reinforce our own negative narrative, we can simply let them go.

What "cloudy" negative thoughts pass through your mind? Jot them down in the cloud below – we'll be using them later!

Getting all the good feels

 JOY DOES NOT SIMPLY HAPPEN TO US.
WE HAVE TO CHOOSE JOY AND KEEP
CHOOSING IT EVERY DAY.
Henri Nouwen

It's all too easy when we're "adulting" to get bogged down by the things that are causing stress or bothering us. If you add a dose of low self-esteem into the mix, you can convince yourself that you're hardwired into dwelling on the negative aspects of your life. But sometimes the solution is easier than you think – it's all about reminding yourself of the little things that bring you joy. And this is different for everyone – whether it's roller-skating round the park, taking the dog on a long, muddy walk, or reminiscing with dear friends. Whatever makes us feel warm inside and connects to our sense of self-worth helps to boost our self-esteem.

Let's try to identify what gives YOU all the good feels. A great way to start this process is to start looking for patterns in your week. Try taking some time each evening to assess how your day made you feel. Ask yourself these questions:

If you could rate your day on a scale of one to ten (one being unhappy and ten being extremely happy), how would you rate it?

Briefly describe your day, what happened to make it a happy/unhappy one? Include even the mundane stuff (you never know, there might be some hidden joy lurking in cleaning the toilet!).

Try to keep some notes in a diary or journal every day for a week. Using your notes, try to identify any patterns. What were you doing on the days that you felt at your best? What didn't make you feel good?

Now, write a list below, using these questions to get you started: What makes you feel amazing? When do you feel most like yourself? When do you laugh most? When do you feel peaceful?

How could you do more of these things? Can you do one of them every day?

Banishing the bad feels

It's normal to have periods in life when everything seems a bit bleurgh, sometimes for no particular reason. Often, these are fleeting – a bit like a grey and miserable day – and we're able to shoo the clouds away and let the sunshine back in again. But sometimes there are specific things we can pinpoint – people, places, situations – which act like a joy vacuum, leaving us feeling bad about ourselves.

Maybe these are obvious, like having to sit next to a toxic work colleague or receiving some negative feedback on a project you've been working on.

But often, it can be something that seems, on the face of it, insignificant to everyone else. To you, however, it's a sure-fire way of making you feel utterly rubbish. Perhaps you hate visiting a particular clothes shop, because you know their products are so teeny-tiny you'll have to buy a size bigger than usual. Or you dread checking social media, because everyone else seems to be living their best life, while you think yours just doesn't stack up.

If we can identify what sucks the joy out of our lives, we can practise damage limitation, which will help us banish the bad feels once and for all.

Take a moment to consider what triggers your low self-esteem. Can you think of two or three situations that are sure to knock it?

Could you change your routine or habits, so you spend less time doing these things, or find a different approach? For example, "I could ask to sit at a different desk at work," or, "I could ask to have my feedback face to face so I have an opportunity to discuss some solutions with my lecturer/boss."

If not, are there changes you could make that would help you feel better about yourself? For example, "I can decide to only visit shops that sell clothes I feel good wearing," or, "I choose not to go on social media if I'm feeling a bit vulnerable."

Freeing up your headspace

Often our heads feel full to bursting with thoughts. Whether you're contemplating what to cook for dinner, what time you need to feed the cat, or planning world domination, this can sometimes seem a bit overwhelming – particularly if they're all jostling for attention at the same time. Besides shouting at your brain to shut up, sometimes it can be useful to write down all the thoughts that are roaming free inside your head, so you have some capacity for reorganizing them, before acting on them or telling them to hit the road!

What's on your mind at this moment? Try writing your thoughts here, on some scrap paper, or in a notebook:

Sometimes, simply writing something down can make us feel better. The process of putting our everyday thoughts into words helps to empty our minds of the clutter, leaving more room for hidden thoughts and emotions to break through.

Now you've offloaded your mental clutter, how do you feel? Perhaps you are relieved, or even happy. Write it down here.

Given time and a little patience, what's really bothering you (which may have been obscured by everyday worries) will often rise to the surface as clear as daylight. Sometimes we need that sense of mental clarity to gain insight into our true feelings. Use the space below to jot down any new emotions you're experiencing.

If you're worried that what you write is uninteresting or makes no sense, remember, you don't need to show anyone — it's for your eyes only. Once you're done, you can keep what you've written, show it to someone else, screw it up and throw it away, or even burn it — the choice is entirely yours.

If writing out your thoughts feels good, you might want to consider keeping a journal. You can write down whatever you feel like, as often as you want. It doesn't need to be anything fancy – a plain notebook works perfectly (although it's a brilliant excuse for new stationery!).

Here's a simple but effective way to use a journal to boost your self-esteem. Draw a line down the centre of the page, like this:

On this side, write your negative thoughts. Don't hold back! For example, "I'm not cut out for my job and I don't know why the company employed me."	**On this side, write answers to those negative thoughts, as if talking to your best friend. For example, "That's not true! You've just had an appraisal and your boss said you're acing it."**

Challenging our thoughts on paper like this can help us to gain perspective. Negative thoughts can often be irrational, overblown and plain irritating, but seeing them in black and white helps to take the emotion out of them. Only then can we recognize how unhelpful they are. The idea is not to invalidate those thoughts, but to interrogate them logically and dispassionately.

Make a self-esteem jar

What is it? A jar full of little self-esteem boosts that you can dip into whenever low self-esteem strikes. Why do I need this? The notes you keep in the jar will remind you of all the positive things in your life and the reasons why you're an amazing human.

You will need: paper, scissors and an empty jar. Plus a healthy attitude towards crafting.

How to make it: cut your paper into lots of squares, 5 cm x 5 cm. On each square, write something that makes you feel good – a memory, an achievement, a compliment, an activity you love to do or that brings you joy, an event you're looking forward to, something you did to help another person, an uplifting line from a favourite book, film or song that always inspires laughter or happiness... whatever makes you feel warm inside.

Our family day at the beach	Setting a new personal best time in a cycling race	"You're the best friend in the world"

The day I brought my rescue pet home for the first time	Helping the local charity reach their fundraising target

Now fold each square and put it in the jar. Whenever you feel down, take out a random square and it will give you a little self-esteem boost!

Making sense of mindfulness

Mindfulness might seem like a recent phenomenon. Perhaps you've seen it mentioned online or on television, or even in a local healthcare setting. However, it's not just a trendy buzzword that pops up frequently in the media or in adult colouring books. Mindfulness has been used as a holistic approach to stress and anxiety for centuries. But how many of us actually know what it is? And why is it so popular now?

Originating in Buddhist philosophy and Hindu teachings, mindfulness is a concept that has gained popularity in recent years for its ability to both clear and reboot the mind, and for successfully promoting mental wellness. Researchers have investigated its benefits and found that it has a remarkable effect on the mind and emotions, reducing anxiety, combatting stress and burnout and, crucially, increasing self-esteem.

Mindfulness involves bringing your attention to the present moment – being aware of where you are, what you're doing and how you are feeling, and observing these things without judgement. Sounds simple, right?

It's a skill that gets easier with practice, but if you're willing to try it, mindfulness will equip you with a brilliant tool for tackling low self-esteem. It'll help you effectively navigate and feel comfortable with your feelings and emotions, even when they're difficult.

How to be the champion of mindfulness

You can do almost anything mindfully. You can type mindfully, walk mindfully, stare out of the window mindfully, take a shower mindfully... you get the picture.
  Here's how it works:

1   Consider the view out of your nearest window.

2   Go to the window – find a comfortable stance, whether that's sitting or standing. Give your full attention to what you can see outside. What's happening within the perimeter of the window frame is your whole universe for the next minute.

3   Look carefully at everything, avoiding the use of categories or labels. Instead, aim to notice colours, textures or patterns. For instance, instead of "sky", notice the different shades of blue, white or grey, or for "pavement" notice the mirror-like reflections in the puddles, or the light and shade of the concrete.

4   Don't forget movement – how is the breeze blowing the grass? Is the washing on the line flapping in the wind?

5   Try to look at the world outside your window as though you were seeing it for the first time.

6   If you feel yourself getting distracted by other thoughts, gently steer your attention by noticing a colour or shape to coax yourself back to the present moment.

As with any skill, mindfulness takes a bit of practice. If it feels strange to begin with, don't let that put you off trying again. Sometimes, the only thing standing between you and your goals is a little direction and patience with yourself.

Next, in the space below, take a moment to jot down how your mindfulness practice made you feel. Take your time – there are prompts in the box if you need them.

It felt strange/relaxing/intense/difficult/easy, etc...

My mind feels...

My mind wandered because I was thinking of...

...was distracting me

My body feels...

...caught my attention

I noticed...

I was most focused on...

Feel-good affirmations

Affirmations are short, impactful sentences that encapsulate positive and inspiring ideas. They can be a brilliant tool for changing your thought patterns and overcoming negative self-talk, the idea being that the more you repeat them, the more you'll believe them. Different affirmations work for different people, depending on what you want to achieve, so the best approach is to try a few out – such as the examples below – and see which ones feel right for you.

I am special in my own way

I can do this

My feelings matter

I can say "no"

I deserve to be treated with kindness and respect

My voice deserves to be heard

I am enough

I am successful

I believe in myself

I forgive myself

I respect myself

My body is precious

My views matter

I can do great things

I am strong

I am loved

Only I am in charge of my life

I am grateful to be me

I like who I am

I can do hard things

I am beautiful

The best affirmations are the ones we've written ourselves, because they come from the heart. Use this page to jot down a set of affirmations that are personal to you:

Once you've settled on an affirmation or two that feel like a good fit for you, you could write them on sticky notes and put them somewhere you'll see them every day, such as a mirror, the kitchen worktop or your desk.

Quick and easy self-esteem boosters

These quick and easy self-esteem boosters are perfect feel-good time fillers when you've only got minutes to spare. Have a think about when you could incorporate them into your week and fill in the planners on the following pages to help you schedule time for them. Creating a schedule like this is a brilliant habit to get into, as it makes you more accountable, because guess what? Once it's written down, it's locked in – no excuses!

Go outside and get fresh air – science has found that being immersed in nature boosts our wellbeing – vitamin D from sunlight, reconnecting with our senses and gentle exercise are just some of the benefits. You could even take a quick mindful walk using the mindfulness exercise on page 40.

Smile – even if you're having the day from hell. The physical act of smiling releases endorphins – those handy little feel-good chemicals – so you'll get an instant positivity boost.

Take a deep breath – increasing the oxygen in your body is a simple but effective way to get a confidence boost and enhance your energy levels, while reducing stress and anxiety. Each time you breathe out, your heart rate slows, coming into sync with your breathing. If you have five minutes, go online and find some breathing exercises to follow.

Check your posture! If you're sitting down, sit up straight rather than hunched over, to instantly feel more in control. Stress and anxiety have a sneaky habit of making us hold our bodies in an unnaturally tense way, without us even realizing. So, relax your shoulders and unclench your jaw to gain instant relief.

Tidy up – whether it's one shelf, your desk, or your entire house, tidying up helps to calm anxiety and raise self-esteem. Improving the environment around you (even just a little bit) makes you feel good inside.

Tap into your creativity – whether this is drawing, painting, dancing or making music, being free to create just for the fun of it is a great self-esteem booster, as it allows your mind to relax and escape the daily grind.

Journalling – writing down your thoughts and feelings boosts self-esteem by giving you the space to express yourself and put yourself first, without worrying about the judgement of other people.

Exercise – simply moving your body is a terrific way to feel better about yourself, and you don't need to rush to the gym either, because any movement counts. Hurrah! Exercise brings your focus away from your thoughts and into your body, making it an excellent mindful activity.

Listen to music – music has an amazing effect on our mood and emotions. Which songs make you feel good about yourself? Listen to these when you feel like you need a pick-me-up. You could even make a self-esteem-boosting playlist.

Use the planner to write your daily to-do list and get those boosters booked in! You could set one or two as a weekly goal, or spread a few of the ideas over the course of the week. The best bit? The sense of satisfaction and achievement you'll get when you tick them off!

Weekly Goals

- [ ]
- [ ]
- [ ]
- [ ]
- [ ]
- [ ]

Monday

- [ ]
- [ ]
- [ ]
- [ ]
- [ ]
- [ ]

Tuesday

- [ ]
- [ ]
- [ ]
- [ ]
- [ ]
- [ ]

Wednesday

- [ ] _____
- [ ] _____
- [ ] _____
- [ ] _____
- [ ] _____
- [ ] _____

Thursday

- [ ] _____
- [ ] _____
- [ ] _____
- [ ] _____
- [ ] _____
- [ ] _____

Friday

- [ ] _____
- [ ] _____
- [ ] _____
- [ ] _____
- [ ] _____
- [ ] _____

Saturday

- [ ] _____
- [ ] _____
- [ ] _____
- [ ] _____
- [ ] _____
- [ ] _____

Sunday

- [ ] _____
- [ ] _____
- [ ] _____
- [ ] _____
- [ ] _____
- [ ] _____

You are uniquely you

Who wants to be "normal"? And, anyway, what even is "normal"?! When we have low self-esteem, it's all too easy to fall into the comparison trap – we assess our self-worth in terms of how we measure up against other people, meaning we view our differences in a negative light, rather than a positive one.

But let's flip that on its head for a moment. Why do you care what other people think of you? Do you love your close friends and relatives because they all look and behave the same? Of course not! Rather, it's their quirks, their own unique qualities and their lived experiences that set them apart from others.

And it's no different for you. You are a unique blend of personality, characteristics, experiences, appearance, strengths and weaknesses. No-one can replace you, because no-one *is* you. Let that be your starting point and then carry this belief with you through life.

Dare to be different – which for most of us means simply being ourselves. When you let your true self shine through, you'll find the tribe you're meant to be in.

We only get one life – don't waste it worrying about what other people think!

BE DARING, BE DIFFERENT, BE
IMPRACTICAL, BE ANYTHING THAT
WILL ASSERT INTEGRITY OF PURPOSE
AND IMAGINATIVE VISION AGAINST
THE PLAY-IT-SAFERS, THE CREATURES
OF THE COMMONPLACE, THE SLAVES
OF THE ORDINARY.

Cecil Beaton

What makes you unique? Maybe you're an absolute dab-hand at solving a Rubik's cube or you have an overriding passion for giant pandas. Maybe you're obsessed with ghosts, fairies and ancient folklore, or perhaps you have a uniquely warm and empathetic personality. Or you might just be you – and that's perfect.

Use the space below to write down some of the character traits, experiences, tastes, hobbies, habits, passions and perspectives that make you uniquely *you*.

It's good to talk

Low self-esteem can make it tricky to start a conversation about how we're really feeling, even with people we're close to. That's because we manage to convince ourselves that our feelings don't matter and no-one cares. When we lack confidence in our self-worth, the easiest option is to clam up, but being able to talk openly about our feelings is a powerful tool for raising our self-esteem. Sharing how we're really feeling with a loved one or someone we trust gives us the opportunity to gain additional support from someone who knows and understands us.

Remember – we don't normally hesitate to tell someone if we're physically unwell or in pain, and we need help and support. This is no different. It may not be as obvious, but if you're struggling with your feelings and it's affecting your everyday life, the issue is just as valid a talking point as a physical illness.

Here are a few ways you could start a conversation about feelings and mental health:

Can I just offload for a minute, please?

I'm going to find this hard, but can I tell you something?

I've noticed I'm struggling with some feelings lately...

This feels awkward, but I need your help.

I read something that's really made me think – can I share it with you?

Could you listen to me for a bit?

Can I talk to you about something personal?

Who can I talk to?

Think about the person (or people) in your life who you find it easiest to talk to. Write down their names here.

Emotions can be messy, complicated and confusing, and it's not always easy to describe how you're feeling, particularly in the moment. Sometimes, it helps to make notes first to order your thoughts. If you can't think of one word to describe how you're feeling, just use several – as long as they make some sort of sense to the listener! What does it feel like inside your head right now? What does it make you want to do or say? If you think it would help you to make notes, use the space below to write down a rough draft of what's on your mind.

If you don't have anyone that you feel comfortable talking to, check the resources on page 155 – you're not alone and there is help available.

Gratitude journalling

Reminding ourselves of the things we're grateful for helps us to focus on the positives – the idea being that no matter how difficult life gets, there is always something to feel grateful for. Some days, this can be a real challenge and you might just appreciate having made it through the day alive. But being able to find something to value about a shockingly tough 24 hours can help to strengthen your resilience, enabling you to deal with any rough times you might face in the future more effectively.

Without stopping to think too much, note down three things you're grateful for today:

1 _____

_____

2 _____

_____

3 _____

_____

If you're stuck, think of something you're grateful to have, something you're grateful already happened and someone you're grateful to have in your life.

What are the benefits of keeping a gratitude journal/diary?

⬤ It can help you to banish the negative parts of your day from your thoughts and focus on the positive bits, which will give your self-esteem a boost.

⬤ Daily gratitude journalling before bed can help you end the day on a positive note, encouraging you to relax and fall asleep more easily.

⬤ It can enable you to gain clarity to recognize the things you need more of in your life, as well as what you can do without!

⬤ It will help you learn more about yourself – and becoming more self-aware is a key aspect of raising your self-esteem.

⬤ You can be truly open about how you feel, without fear of judgement.

⬤ On a day when your self-esteem is at rock bottom, you can reread your journal to readjust your attitude and remind yourself of all the good things in your life.

Turn the page for a ready-made gratitude diary!

Gratitude Tracker

Date:

Monday

Tuesday

Wednesday

Thursday

Friday

Saturday

Sunday

You are who you are, and that will always be enough

Worrying never did anyone any good – fact. And since there's a lot of information in this book about raising your self-esteem, and you might think self-esteem is something you're not particularly good at "doing", this page is here to provide all the reassurance you need.

It's OK to have low self-esteem. It's also OK to feel sad, mad, glad or whatever emotion you're experiencing right now. It's even OK to feel like sticking two fingers up to the world and everyone in it.

So, the point is – don't worry. Your end goal is not to move mountains and you're definitely not aiming to have "perfect" self-esteem (that's just not possible, unless you're some sort of robot who is preprogrammed to "permanently perfect" mode).

People mess up and do crazy, stupid things. We all have flaws – some easier to live with than others. The aim is to adjust the way you think about yourself, so that your self-talk becomes more compassionate, and you're able to cut yourself some slack every now and again. Then, when life does throw you a curve ball, your thoughts will naturally be of the comforting, rather than berating, variety.

Got it? Super... now read on.

My self-esteem emergency rescue kit

Now we've looked at some of the ways you can give your self-esteem a quick boost, it's time to pull it all together in one handy place. Say hello to your self-esteem emergency rescue kit! Use the kit for a quick recharge when your self-esteem is flagging and needs assistance.

Think back to the boosters we've talked about in this section. Use the spaces on this page and the next to write down the things that will give your self-esteem a prod in the right direction – you can come back to it any time you need.

I can talk to...

An idea that helps me...
(E.g. I've got this)

An activity that helps me...
(E.g. mindfulness)

Remember that...
(E.g. you are enough)

A person it feels good to be around...

My favourite affirmation...

A song that fills me with confidence...

A hobby or interest that energizes me...

PART 3

How to tackle negative self-talk

We can be our own worst critics sometimes. We make a mistake and at the drop of a hat, out of nowhere, a little voice pops into our heads reminding us how useless we are – "I never could do that right" or "I messed up, so I'm not surprised they don't like me" or "I've said the wrong thing AGAIN" and so on, ad infinitum.

The problem is, this sort of negative chatter has a sneaky habit of sounding plausible – so we just accept it as gospel. You may even define your negative voice as being rational – after all, it's your in-built fault finder, and since we're all flawed in one way or another (as already discussed) it's perfectly acceptable to give yourself a hard time, because then you can learn from it, right? But there's a difference between self-reflection and engaging in a negative dialogue with yourself. Negative self-talk isn't constructive – in fact, it's very often *destructive* – and it seldom motivates us to make any changes.

In this chapter, we'll look at how to recognize negative self-talk and the impact of a critical voice on our self-esteem. We'll also be offering tips and activities to help you turn the volume down on your negative chatter, while cranking up the self-love instead.

What is self-talk?

Self-talk is the way we talk to ourselves – also known as our inner voice. Most people don't usually vocalize their self-talk (unless they are a character in one of Shakespeare's plays). It's the chat we have with ourselves, in our heads, every day. It might go something like this: "Right, time to think about dinner. But first I need to just do this one thing. Jeez, what is that terrible smell! Why are there biscuit crumbs everywhere? Great, now I'll have to hoover..." etc, etc.

Everyone has self-talk – it's perfectly normal. The self-talk we're concerned with here is *negative* self-talk. That's the voice you hear when you make a mistake or something bad happens that you think is your fault, even if it isn't. If you have low self-esteem, that voice is probably a bit of a jerk.

What you might not realize just yet is that voice isn't the truth, and it's certainly not a reflection of how other people perceive you. With hard work and patience, you can turn your self-talk bully into your best friend.

Getting acquainted with your self-talk

Take five minutes to sit quietly by yourself and tune in to your self-talk. Try to filter out the mindless chatter about what's for dinner and whether you'll get to binge watch a box set later. Can you hear your inner voice? Is it in jerk-mode right now?

Perhaps you got something wrong at work today or you're worrying about body image. What does that inner voice have to say right now? If you feel comfortable, you can write it here:

(Now you can do what you like with what you've just written. Keep it, scribble it out, throw it on a bonfire... but the best response is to write something kinder about yourself in bold letters.)

You can spot negative self-talk by the way it's always repeating itself. It will use the same words or tell you the same negative narrative about yourself, over and over. It's a bit like a stuck record and rarely – if ever – reflects reality.

Tell the negative committee
that meets inside your head
to sit down and shut up.

Ann Bradford

Thoughts are not the same as facts

When we only have our own negative thoughts for company – and we're stuck listening to the same old narrative day in, day out – we start to believe them. What we're not very good at is stopping to see whether that niggling, unhelpful voice in our minds is right or not.

Thoughts are just thoughts – they aren't facts. The same applies to your negative self-talk. Thinking or telling yourself something doesn't make it true. For instance, perhaps you've convinced yourself that you've failed an exam and your destructive self-talk is telling you it's a dead cert, because you're too stupid to pass. Thinking that won't change the outcome – after all, it's now out of your control – but it might change the way you feel about yourself.

If you get stuck in a negative frame of mind and your self-talk is reinforcing this, it's OK... and happens to everyone. The trick is not to try to stop these thoughts, but simply take less notice of them. Acknowledge them, yes, but then tell them to push off!

Fact-check your negative self-talk

Next time negative thoughts start building up in your mind, try asking yourself these questions:

- Am I being fair to myself? (E.g. it's not fair to tell myself I'm stupid, I wouldn't say that to someone else.)

- Is it helpful for me to think this? (E.g. it's not helpful to tell myself I'm too stupid to even try, because I'm holding myself back.)

- Is it likely to be true? (E.g. it's not likely that I'm stupid – no-one has ever called me that except me!)

- Is it based on fact? (E.g. "I'm stupid" is not a fact – I can't back it up. I've done stupid things in the past because of poor judgement, but that doesn't mean I'm unintelligent.)

- What facts prove this thought wrong? (E.g. I have learned a new skill before and mastered it, and I'm successful in my job.)

- Would I say this to my best friend? (E.g. if not, why am I saying it to myself?)

Use the next page to write your answers. Remember, the more you challenge your negative thought patterns, the easier it will become to dismiss them as soon as they begin to make themselves heard. Fact!

What's the worst that could happen... and the best?

As we've discussed, thoughts aren't facts – so if that's the case, you're free to replace them with whatever you like! And since it's the *negative* thoughts that affect self-esteem, it makes sense that the best way to pick yourself up when you're feeling down is to replace that negativity with something positive. Low self-esteem is fuelled by negative thoughts, and negative thoughts are fuelled by negative self-talk, which then feeds back into low self-esteem, and so on and so forth – you get the picture. When your mind is full to bursting with negativity like this, it's important that you rebalance it with a dose of positivity to help raise your self-esteem.

Here is an exercise you can try next time you're in a negative mindset.

What's the worst that could happen? Let's briefly go into full-on catastrophe mode. We won't stay here long, as it can be a dark and unpleasant place, but research shows that if you can express your insecurities and anxieties, whether in a journal, speaking to someone you trust or just admitting them to yourself, it can help the rationalization process.

Use the space below and in the box opposite, to write what's been bothering you. There are some prompts to help. When you've finished, see opposite for the next step.

"I'm really worried that _____ **will happen."**

"I can't stop thinking about _____ **."**

"Thinking about _____ **is making me anxious."**

And what's the best that could happen? Take a moment to imagine what it would be like if your worst-case scenario had a positive outcome. Close your eyes and visualize yourself doing well. Picture how that would feel and what it would look like.

For example, if your worst-case scenario is something like this...

"I can't stop thinking about my job interview. I'll say something stupid and the panel will think I'm a total idiot. Then I won't get the job and I'll have the embarrassment of telling my family, who'll think I'm a failure."

Swap the negative thought for this...

"I've been thinking a lot about my job interview, but that's OK because it's giving me a chance to explore how I really feel about this opportunity. I'll be super-confident and ask loads of questions, because this is a chance for me to interview the company and make sure I'm a good fit for it. It will also be useful practice for any future interviews, so I can use it to develop my skills, too. I think this could go quite well."

Now have a go yourself in the space below, adding as much detail as you can.

Aim to look at a situation realistically and with a balanced perspective. Bad things do happen – that's life, unfortunately – but positive thinkers choose to view challenging situations as a chance to learn and grow, rather than convince themselves the world is against them. If you get into the habit of thinking more positively, you'll begin to believe and trust in yourself a little more each time, and your self-esteem will start to grow.

How the past can shape your self-esteem

Among the many and varied functions our amazing human brain copes with on a day-to-day basis, it's also rather good at keeping us safe. Remember that time you reached over a boiling kettle and burned your hand in the jet of steam coming from the spout? You almost certainly won't make that mistake again, because your brain remembers the yowl of pain and blistered skin that were the unhappy consequence of that incident. Ever since, your brain has been making sure you're extra-careful around boiling kettles.

But what's that got to do with self-esteem?

Events in the past that have made us feel embarrassed or rejected make just as clear an imprint on our brains as physical pain, such as a burn. So, if you've had a bad experience in the past, your brain will make sure you're wary of the things that remind it of that. It will trick you into thinking it's not worth trying again, just in case you get hurt. Low self-esteem is your brain's way of trying to keep you safe from things that happened before.

The past cannot be changed and it can be difficult to let it go, but accepting it and moving on is key to nurturing healthy self-esteem. Try not to let previous negative experiences shape the person you are – remember that events *happen* to you, they are not part of you.

Are your thoughts holding you back?

Feelings of low self-esteem can develop when the brain reacts to negative thoughts with what psychologists call "thinking errors". These are negative ways of thinking about yourself and the world around you that sound totally convincing. But often, these thoughts simply aren't real. In fact, they're a bit like a story written by your brain – one that's riddled with inaccuracies and completely lacking in facts. Only you can choose whether to believe the narrative or not.

Here are the most common thinking errors and how to spot them:

All-or-nothing thinking: I can never be happy. I'm a failure at life.

Over-generalizing: if one thing goes wrong, everything will go wrong as a result.

Focusing on the negative: if one thing goes wrong, that's the only thing I can think about, despite other things going right. Difficulty in moving past the problem.

Fortune-telling: I know I'll fail. I'll embarrass myself.

Mind-reading: I know everyone will think badly of me. He thinks I'm stupid.

Catastrophizing: one mistake will ruin everything. She didn't answer my call, something bad must have happened.

Magnified thinking: the things I like about myself aren't important. I forgot to get dinner in, I'm the worst partner ever.

Negative comparison: she's way more successful than me.

Unrealistic expectations: I should be perfect at everything, all the time.

Putting yourself down: I'm a failure. I'm a horrible person.

Do any of these sound like your self-talk? Draw a circle around any that you recognize. Once you learn to identify your thinking errors, you can begin to challenge those thoughts by gathering evidence that will paint a more realistic picture. Changing how you think about yourself takes a lot of effort initially, but with practice you'll notice big changes to your self-esteem.

Responding to negative self-talk

It's OK to have negative thoughts – in fact, it's perfectly normal. Not only do they keep us safe ("I'm no good at ice-skating, so I'll have to go slow or I'll have an accident"), but occasionally they can be useful – for instance, to help motivate us when we're trying to achieve a goal ("I'm really disappointed in myself because I failed that test, but I'll try harder next time"). But if your self-talk has become more harmful than helpful, it's probably necessary to reassess how you respond to your inner critic.

The trick is to understand how your mind works, so you'll be able to identify why a specific thought is floating around your head at a particular time. This way, you can filter out the useful chatter from the useless chatter.

For example, if you're thinking negatively about your body image, it could be because you were idly scrolling through social media and a celebrity influencer was showing off their new "bikini body". Or maybe you accidentally overheard someone else talking negatively about their body. We exist in a world full of messages, some of which our minds absorb and some they don't. For healthy self-esteem, we need to be able to differentiate between the messages that are worth listening to and those that aren't.

Swap your negative thoughts for positive ones

There are a few ways you can reduce the impact of negative thoughts on your self-esteem, but one of the most effective is to swap your negative thoughts for positive ones. Sounds simple, doesn't it? But in practice, this technique takes a little time to get used to, because you need to catch the negative thought before it has a chance to do any damage and then give it a positive spin. The good news is, once you've got into the habit, you'll do it without even realizing!

So, what's the secret method?

All you need to do is take your next negative thought and give it a nudge (or a shove, in some cases) towards positivity, like this:

I'm stupid → I'm finding this quite challenging

I should be able to do this → I need more training

I look like an idiot → I look like a beginner

I can never do anything right → It's tricky, but I'm going to persevere

I can't do this, it's pointless trying → I can try my best and it's OK if I fail

I should give up, I wish I'd never started → I'm going to take this one step at a time. I believe in myself

Now it's time to put it into practice. Each time a thinking error or negative thought threatens to bring down your self-esteem, write it here. Can you push it towards some positivity? Take your time and, if it's not working out for you right now, you can always come back to it later.

Break the negative circuit with your body

Sometimes negative self-talk sounds like an endless cycle of irritating chatter. It's a little like an unwelcome guest in your head – one who simply won't shut up! Next time your negativity won't take the hint, try shifting your focus to your body for a few moments – it might just be enough to break the circuit and kick your negative chatter into touch.

Take a deep breath through your nose, right down into your belly. Feel your lungs expanding and enjoy the sensation of them emptying as you exhale slowly through your nose. Repeat three times.

Let your arms go limp and swing them sideways and upward, then to the other side in a semi-circle. Repeat three times.

Stretch up to the ceiling, as if you're reaching for a high shelf, then flop down to touch your toes. Repeat three times.

Breathe deeply, bringing your attention to the centre of your chest. Put your hands on your ribcage and feel it move up and down. Keep your focus on your chest as you feel your heart rate slow with every breath, in and out. Continue for six breaths.

Breaking it down

Low self-esteem can make it easy for us to feel overwhelmed when we're faced with a challenge. It convinces us it's not even worth trying because we're doomed to fail, or that we're too stupid to deal with something so complex and time-consuming.

The trick is to break the challenge down into smaller goals, which you can take at a pace that feels comfortable for you. The idea is that each step in the process will bring you closer to your main goal, but in a much more manageable (and ultimately less self-esteem crushing) way.

Here's how it works:

Take learning to knit. You don't start off by whipping up a fancy cardigan that wouldn't be out of place on a catwalk. The first steps are to understand how to hold the knitting needles and read a pattern. Then you might want to learn a little bit about wool and the best type for your design, as well as how to make stitches. Only after you've understood your chosen material, mastered working with your knitting needles, making the stitches and where to start the pattern, will you be able to knit something tangible. You'll probably drop a stitch or two and your cardigan might have more holes than a packet of Swiss cheese, but with a little time and patience, the things you found difficult in the beginning will become easier and each skill you learn will build on the last, in turn creating new goals for you to aim for.

Your turn! What challenges or tasks feel a bit daunting to you right now? Perhaps you're preparing for an important project at work and it's making you anxious, or you might be planning some home improvements and you don't know where to start. Use the ladder below to break your main goal into manageable steps.

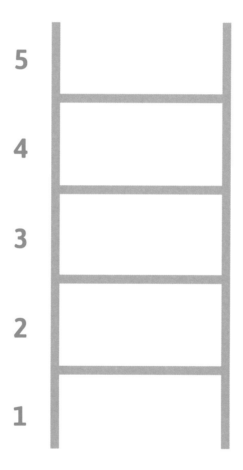

Keeping track of your mood

Keeping track of your mood is a great way to help you spot patterns in your emotions and identify what might be having a negative impact on your state of mind.
  Why is this important?

- It can help you identify external and internal triggers that cause mood changes and/or affect your self-esteem.

- You'll learn more about how factors such as sleep, diet, exercise and daily activities affect how you're feeling.

- Mood tracking can help you develop coping techniques to deal with negative thoughts.

- You'll gain a better understanding of your shifts in mood and, hopefully, a better understanding of yourself!

A quick and easy way to do this is by filling in a daily mood chart. The great news is, there's a ready-to-go chart on the next two pages – you're welcome!

How to fill in your mood chart:

Simple – just make a note of how you're feeling every day, remembering to jot down which activities or tasks you were doing that may have triggered any negative thoughts. You could also record anything you did to alleviate those feelings, such as exercise or mindfulness, and whether it helped you feel better.

Sunday	Monday
Morning:	Morning:
Afternoon:	Afternoon:
Evening:	Evening:
Notes:	Notes:
Tuesday	**Wednesday**
Morning:	Morning:
Afternoon:	Afternoon:
Evening:	Evening:
Notes:	Notes:

Thursday	Friday
Morning:	Morning:
Afternoon:	Afternoon:
Evening:	Evening:
Notes:	Notes:

Saturday
Morning:
Afternoon:
Evening:
Notes:

Top mood-tracking tips

- Be honest with yourself. While it might feel uncomfortable recording how you really feel when you're down, try to be as candid as possible.

- Don't forget to record the positives, too! While you're trying to get a sense of the reasons for your negativity, it's just as important to note when you're feeling at your best, so that you capture the whole picture.

- Try to check in at regular intervals and incorporate this into your daily routine, so it'll become easier for you to remember to do it.

Throw out your negative thoughts

When it comes to stamping out the negativity in your life, there's something really satisfying about the act of physically throwing those thoughts away or destroying them completely. Symbolically ridding yourself of thoughts and beliefs you no longer want or need can be a powerful way to realign your thinking. The theory goes that if you create something that exists outside of yourself that represents these thoughts – such as notes, drawings, scrap paper, a journal, etc. – and then let these things go (or better yet, destroy them), it can help your mind to release the negativity.

Not convinced? Here's the science. In a study conducted by Ohio State University, a group of people were asked to write down negative thoughts on slips of paper and then later throw the papers away. Another group was asked to do a similar thing, only they had to keep the slips of paper. The result? Researchers discovered the act of throwing out a negative thought literally helps discard it mentally.

It's time to locate the nearest bin...

PART 4

How self-esteem can affect your actions

In the same way that your self-esteem is reflected in your thoughts and feelings, it also has a profound impact on your day-to-day life. It affects the choices you make and determines what you consider yourself to be capable (and worthy) of doing.

In fact, every part of your life can be affected by your self-esteem – whether that's reflected in your choice of partner, how you cope with the demands of your job, how much self-care you allow yourself or whether you're confident trying new things. Many areas of your life are, to some extent, out of your control – but your self-esteem isn't one of them! Only you can control how you approach life, and a healthy self-esteem is crucial to making the most of it. In this chapter, we'll be exploring the ways in which self-esteem impacts on your everyday actions, how you can learn to break a pattern of low self-esteem and how to work towards positive change.

How to spot low self-esteem in your behaviour

We may not always notice how our self-esteem affects our thoughts and feelings, but the way it influences our actions and behaviours can be more obvious. Here are some examples of self-esteem manifesting itself in our everyday lives:

Avoidance: avoiding or choosing not to do something because it challenges you.

Dee would love to join the new history club in her hometown, but she's worried the other members will be degree-educated experts and look down on her for leaving school at sixteen, so she chooses not to go at all.

Hiding: keeping the things that make us different a secret from others.

Ishmael likes reading and writing poetry. He thinks his friends would laugh if they found out, so he keeps his hobby a secret.

Perfectionism: trying to be perfect at everything, all the time.

Claire has no opportunity to relax at the weekends because she spends all her time either working or looking after her family. She thinks she's failing in all areas because her time is spread so thinly and that her friends will judge her for not being able to cope with the demands of her life.

Passivity: always trying to please other people and not feeling able to say "no" to things, even when you don't want to do them.

Simon lets his manager take advantage of his hard work ethic by accepting extra projects, even though he doesn't really have the time, and it's making him stressed. He's hoping it will impress his boss, even though it means his workload has become unmanageable and the stress is making him feel ill.

Aggression: treating others in an overbearing, intimidating or hurtful way, to make them feel bad about themselves.

Every time Jena visits her daughter Kinga, she can't help but point out how disappointed she is in her and what she should be doing with her life, despite the fact Kinga is a grown woman.

Attention-seeking: trying to get other people to tell you that you're a good or interesting person; trying to make people feel sorry for you; doing risky or shocking things so people take notice of you.

Andy tells lies about himself because he thinks it will make him more popular. He pretends he has met lots of celebrities and sports stars through his job in the media, because he knows this will impress his friends.

Do any of these traits sound familiar? If that's the case, it's nothing to worry about – we all have little negative characteristics that pop up in a minor way every now and again. Most of the time, they don't cause too much harm, but regularly behaving in this way damages our self-esteem in the long run.

This is because in order to make strong, positive connections, your mind needs to have positive experiences of you being the best version of yourself. It's about teaching your brain that even if you make a mistake, say something you regret or can't do something at the first attempt, your friends and family will still be there for you – *you'll* still be there for yourself – and you can cope with the negative feelings that might arise. If you're struggling to be your true self and you don't practise authenticity, your mind won't get a chance to make new neural pathways. It's the destructive behaviours identified on the last couple of pages that fuel your low self-esteem pathways.

Can you think of a time when low self-esteem affected the way you acted? What happened?

If you could go back and live that moment again, would you do anything differently?

Pressing the pause button

Managing the complex web of emotions that we humans come equipped with is challenging. And to make things that bit trickier, we often can't stop ourselves reacting hastily to certain situations. Perhaps this sounds familiar...

- **Something/someone triggers your emotions**
- **You react negatively**
- **Time passes**
- **You calm down**
- **You regret reacting negatively**

We've all been there – the argument with a loved one that ends in tears and a stony silence, or the time you were juggling too many tasks and snapped at the kids because they were making so much noise. It's a story that's as old as the hills and gets played out repeatedly, all over the world. Nothing will change that. But there are steps we can take to lessen the negative impact in this type of scenario.

Only you can control your behaviour and how you respond to certain situations. This is great news, because it means you have the power to change things for the better. And the way to do that is to learn how to press pause on yourself.

Low self-esteem behaviours usually happen when a negative situation has triggered negative emotions. Pressing pause on yourself means recognizing that you're feeling one – or even several – big emotion(s), taking a deep breath and just staying with the feeling. You can use mindfulness here, which you learned about in Part 2.

Here's how to put it into practice:

- Pause: stop what you're doing.
- Take a deep breath.
- Tell yourself (either aloud, in your head or written down): "I'm feeling _____ ."
- Notice how that emotion feels in your body and simply sit with it for a moment.
- If you feel the urge to turn to one of the low self-esteem behaviours, you could say, think or write: "I really want to _____ ," but don't act on it. This way, you're acknowledging how you feel, but without the negative repercussions of following it through.
- Take three more deep breaths.

Getting used to pausing can be initially challenging but stick with it. The strength of human emotions and the primal fight-or-flight reaction to most tricky situations means the urge to react or respond is sometimes very strong. But pausing really is the most positive thing you can do.

Pausing gives you the opportunity to take a step back, get some distance from the situation, decide on a positive reaction or response, and then move forward. This is empowering for your self-esteem, because you are taking control of your decisions and reactions, instead of allowing your triggers to determine this for you.

Being assertive

Assertiveness often gets a bit of a bad rap. It's the one trait that seems to find itself being used, completely unjustifiably, by people who just want to get their own way regardless of other people's feelings. This isn't assertiveness. This is called bullying.

Ironically, if more of us *were* assertive, we'd be better equipped to kick the rude people into touch! Assertiveness allows us to make clear our wants, needs, points of view and boundaries, while simultaneously acknowledging and respecting the same in others. It's the ultimate expression of self-respect and high self-esteem.

Choosing not to let low self-esteem affect how you act takes a certain amount of bravery, and often it's our low self-esteem that prevents us from expressing what we really want in life. Perhaps you're afraid of confrontation, or think that speaking your mind will lose you friends. Or maybe you just don't know how to communicate your feelings confidently. Fortunately, assertiveness is a skill that can be learned. We can improve how we assert ourselves through the activities in this section, as well as by putting our assertiveness into practice in our own lives.

- **Assertiveness means expressing clearly and truthfully what you like and dislike, rather than following the crowd or "people-pleasing".**

- **Assertiveness means being honest about your feelings, rather than staying silent and expecting others to read your mind.**

- **Assertiveness means saying sorry when you have hurt someone, rather than blaming them or pretending it didn't happen.**

- **Assertiveness means persevering after making a mistake, rather than giving up.**

Assertiveness in action

Can you think of a habit you have that is a result of low self-esteem? You could revisit the earlier journalling pages to get ideas. Or perhaps you have a situation in mind that would involve you standing up for yourself and communicating your true feelings, but you haven't quite found the courage to do it yet.

Think about how you could use assertiveness in this situation and write about it here:

Practice makes perfect assertiveness

When someone is being assertive, they tend to project confidence through their bodies, as well as through their words. They maintain eye contact, have good posture, use a calm and even tone, and use their body language to communicate effectively.

You too can use your body to practise being assertive. Research shows that rehearsing non-verbal assertive movements alongside verbal communication helps to develop resilience in moments of panic or shutdown. Just as you did with positive thoughts, the more you practise speaking and moving your body in an assertive way, the more natural it will feel to model this behaviour the next time you need to make your feelings known.

You'll need someone to do this exercise with, such as a partner or trusted friend. Stand face to face with each other and bring both hands up to touch palms.

Think about a situation in which you want to act assertively. Imagine what you will say. Say it aloud and push the other person's hands. They should stand firm and gently resist your pushing.

Now we've explored how to project assertiveness through your body, it's time to think about how to convey assertiveness through your words. One of the most important parts of being assertive is taking ownership of – and communicating – your feelings, opinions and behaviours, so using the right language is crucial.

One of the best ways to do this is to practise using "I" statements. Doing this avoids placing the blame on the person you are speaking to (therefore avoiding a negative reaction) or giving up your own agency because you've transferred it to the other person. For example:

"When you _____ , I _____ ."

Fill in the speech bubbles below with your own "I" statements, based on what you'd like to communicate assertively. The first one is done for you to get you started!

When you make a mess and expect me to tidy it up, it means I have less time to relax and do things I enjoy, and then I feel resentful. I feel as if my time is less important than yours.

Try something new

When was the last time you tried something new? If you have to think too hard, it's definitely been too long – and if this is the case, there's a good chance low self-esteem is to blame. The problem is, it can be tricky to motivate yourself if you've convinced yourself that you're incompetent or a chronic under-performer, but conversely this then becomes a self-fulfilling prophecy. To overcome feelings of low self-worth, you need to trust in the knowledge that you can do more than you think.

You don't have to dive straight in and try bungee jumping or lion-taming – unless you want to, of course – but taking some small, achievable steps towards a new adventure or skill will help to raise your self-esteem up several notches. Teach yourself to crochet or learn a different language. Build a model aeroplane or take up playing tennis. Do whatever makes you feel good and gives you that all-important dose of self-belief. You don't need to become an expert; you just need to *try*.

In time, you will learn there is literally nothing you can't do when you believe in yourself. Even lion-taming...

What's in it for me?

● **Trying something new will develop your inner strength and resilience.**

● **You'll find joy in the act of discovering a new experience.**

● **You'll be practising a growth mindset, which is vital to help you embrace life's challenges.**

● **You might just tap into a hidden talent you never knew you had – anything's possible!**

Be fearless in trying
new things, whether
they are physical, mental,
or emotional, since being
afraid can challenge you
to go to the next level.

Rita Wilson

PART 5

Taking good care of yourself

When life is demanding, it's easy to slip into auto-pilot mode. Looking after your self-esteem probably doesn't figure much in your daily chores, on top of the important life admin you also need to remember. In fact, it's probably bottom of your priorities – if you're even aware of it at all! But imagine for a moment that looking after your self-esteem *was* on your daily to-do list – what would that look like?

A vital part of cultivating healthy self-esteem is taking care of yourself. Surprisingly, this doesn't come naturally to many of us, particularly if we spend much of our time caring for small people, a partner, or other family members. It's also difficult if you have low self-esteem. Perhaps you feel as if you don't deserve to spend time nurturing your well-being, or you feel guilty for prioritizing your needs above your family's. But putting yourself first every now and again isn't selfish – it's crucial to your overall well-being. And this can only be beneficial for your self-esteem.

When was the last time you checked in with yourself? If it's been so long you can't remember, it's time to do something about it! Read on to find out how to recharge those inner batteries and promote a positive mindset by taking good care of yourself.

Me, myself and I

It's never been easier to interact with other people. And we're absolutely spoilt for choice when it comes to choosing how to connect with friends, family, colleagues and those who share our interests. We can email, text, phone, join an online chat room or forum, video call, comment on social media posts – the list is endless. Knowing that connection is available at the touch of a button is often comforting, but it's also important for us to have time where we're alone with our own thoughts for company, without being distracted by other people.

Spending time on your own is crucial for healthy self-esteem. It gives you the chance to get to know yourself and not worry about pleasing anyone else. You might be thinking this sounds lonely, particularly if you're used to being surrounded by others, but you'd be surprised how liberating it can be. Here's just some of the benefits:

- There's no pressure to be anything other than yourself, so you won't feel you have to perform.

- You can explore your thoughts, feelings, passions, likes, dislikes, views and opinions away from any outside influence, which means you can get to know your authentic self.

- It can give you a chance to work through problems in your head without distraction.

- It'll give you the space to plan new opportunities and explore fresh possibilities for your life.

- It'll help you recharge mentally, so you can rejoin a hectic society with a clear head.

- You'll get to spend time with someone awesome – YOU!

What do you like to do alone? Add your own!

Reading

Walking

Running

Journalling

Listening to music

Crocheting

Gardening

Painting

My relaxation toolbox

We all know that a hectic life equals high stress levels. Whether it's the demands of a job or looking after the house and everyone in it – or both – taking time out to relax has never been more important. Yet so many of us struggle to find the time and space to just breathe and pause life for a moment. If you're having problems unwinding, try one of these simple relaxation tools. Whether you've got five minutes to spare or a whole hour, putting everyday life to one side and focusing on yourself will help rebalance your mind and body.

You have permission to ignore the dishes and that email that's just landed in your inbox....

And breathe...

You don't need to be a yoga or meditation expert to master deep-breathing. Just take ten minutes of quiet time and enjoy using the power of your breath to calm yourself. Find a comfortable spot and place one palm on your stomach. Breathe in deeply through your nose and feel your chest expanding. Then exhale through your mouth until your chest falls. Concentrate on the rise and fall of your breath for 10 minutes – set a timer if you need to.

Zoning out

This one can be tricky when we're surrounded by all the hustle and bustle of everyday life, but stick with it! If your environment isn't particularly calming, find a place that is. You could sit beneath a tree or by the window – anywhere that works for you. Then just let your head empty. You could people watch, or focus on an object further away, or simply gaze into the distance. It's daydreaming, but with purpose!

If you can't escape your environment, add something soothing to your space, such as an aromatherapy candle, a hot herbal drink or even a potted plant. Often, it's the smallest things that make the biggest difference.

Healing with your hands and feet

Swap wringing your hands with worry for a little TLC instead. Just a five-minute hand massage can help relieve stress and anxiety.

Rub your favourite cream into your palms – bonus benefits if it's an aromatherapy lotion! Massage each joint and the webbing between each finger. Clench and release your fists, then flex your fingers five times. The stretch will help relieve tension, particularly if you use a keyboard regularly.

For your feet, grab a ball – tennis, golf, the kids' bouncy ball, even the dog's ball (if it's not too grim) – and simply roll it gently under the arch of your foot. If you find any tense spots, stop and apply a little pressure there.

Yoga

Yoga isn't just about physical health and flexibility. Research shows yoga is just as beneficial for your mental wellbeing, due to its meditative and non-competitive qualities – which is fantastic news for your self-esteem. It also improves your connection with yourself. In fact, the word *yoga* comes from the root word *yuj*, which means *to bind*, so it's all about nurturing that all-important relationship with yourself.

Starting your day with some simple yoga stretches will help you feel more awake and positive first thing in the morning. It's also brilliant for helping you get in the right frame of mind for a decent night's sleep. If you practise regularly, you'll gradually feel your muscles become more supple and the stretches easier, bringing a sense of achievement.

Try these poses as a starting point, and don't forget to breathe slowly and evenly for maximum benefit:

Child's pose: great for stretching your upper body. Hold for five breaths in and out.

Cat-cow stretch: inhale and drop your belly for cow's pose and then, as you exhale, round your spine for cat pose. Repeat five times for loosening a tense spine.

Thread the needle: this spinal twist is fabulous for working out those kinks! Hold for three to five breaths on each side.

Downward dog: either hold for three to five breaths, or bend each leg slightly in turn for a back-of-the-leg stretch.

Social media and you

Social media is a bit like carrying around all your loved ones, friends, acquaintances, favourite celebrities, influencers, brands and global news – in your pocket. The problem is, pockets aren't very big and everyone is fighting for space and airtime. While social media has transformed the way we connect with the world around us, it also has the potential to be a toxic environment – particularly if you're feeling vulnerable, struggling with your mental health or have low self-esteem. Users often take to social media when something goes wrong and, before you know it, instead of happy, smiley images of the folk you love, your feed is full of people ranting about politics or moaning about someone else's parking. It's hardly a restful and relaxing place to hang out! It's also a window into other people's lives, and oversharing information has its own set of issues around safeguarding, being judged unfavourably by others and being trolled.

It's easy to blame all of society's ills on social media, but it's not all doom and gloom. Used wisely, social media has allowed us to form and maintain digital relationships in a way we never could before. We can express ourselves and hook up with those who share our hobbies and interests. In essence, we can find our tribe. And that can be just as important to our self-esteem as the other approaches we've discussed. There are only three words you need to remember in relation to social media – "Everything in moderation" – and what's great is that some super-clever people have designed various social media tracker apps to enable you to do just that. These apps help us to understand just how much time we're spending on social media (longer than we think) and allow us to set a limit, so we don't disappear into a social media time-warp – result!

Why do you use social media? How do you feel before you check your feed?

Use the space below to note the reasons you're using social media and how you feel *before* clicking on that familiar icon to access your feed. Perhaps you look forward to seeing what everyone is doing, or maybe it makes you feel a bit apprehensive or anxious. Try to give an honest appraisal of your emotions.

Before going on social media, I feel...

_____

_____

Then, once you're on social media, take a moment to pay attention to how it's making you feel – particularly in relation to your self-esteem. What thoughts are you having? When you've finished writing, rate how high your self-esteem is feeling out of ten, with one being very low and ten being very high.

Whilst on social media, I feel...

_____

_____

Self-esteem rating: ____ / 10

Now you've finished on social media, how do you feel?

After using social media, I feel...

_____

_____

Self-esteem rating: ____ / 10

Find your inner creativity

We've all got a little creativity tucked away inside us. Whether you're a dab hand at dancing or a beginner at the bagpipes, creativity is something everyone can enjoy, irrespective of age and ability. The problem is, when our self-esteem is low, it's difficult for us to have confidence in our own capabilities. But know this – there's no right or wrong way of doing creative activities, which means you can just appreciate the process without worrying whether what you're doing is "good enough". And unless you're planning on sharing your talents with the rest of the world, there's absolutely nothing wrong with keeping your creations to yourself!

Here are some creative ideas to inspire you:

Create a scrapbook of something you're interested in or fill it with positive memories

Learn an instrument (bagpipes optional!)

Sketch a household object or pet (if you can get them to sit still for long enough!)

Write a poem about what you see out of the window

Start collecting something (like vintage postcards or seashells)

Learn bushcraft skills

Write a story using a picture from a magazine as a prompt

Journal your hopes and wishes for the future

Use the planner to keep track of the creative activities you try, and note down how they make you feel beforehand and afterwards. Do they help you relax? Do you feel more positive? Perhaps you've surprised yourself with how capable you are – if so, make sure you write it down!

Creativity Tracker

	Activity	Time spent on activity	How I felt before the activity	How I felt afterwards
Monday				
Tuesday				
Wednesday				
Thursday				
Friday				
Saturday				
Sunday				

Plan a date with yourself

Getting to spend time alone means hanging out with fabulous company, so why not get a date in the diary for some "you time" to look forward to? Put on clothes that make you feel great and treat yourself.

It could be as simple as binge-watching a boxset with a bucket-load of popcorn or going to get your hair done by a fancy stylist. Spending time alone will allow you to nurture the relationship you have with yourself, which is vital for cultivating healthy self-esteem – and thinking of it as a date will put you in the right frame of mind for giving yourself some much-needed TLC.

What will you do to treat yourself?

How did it go? Write about what happened and how you felt:

A different perspective

Being respectful and tolerant of other people's viewpoints is part of life, whether in the classroom, at home, in the workplace or online. But being tolerant doesn't mean going along with the consensus or staying silent about your own views. Instead, it means healthy discussion and open communication with others, where everyone is free to express their opinions on a level playing field.

This is often a test for our self-esteem, because we may feel that our opinions are not worthy of being heard, or we might think that if we disagree with someone then it may compromise our friendship with them. Low self-esteem can also make us reluctant to say what we really think, so we decide it's easier – and less likely to become confrontational – if we simply agree.

This is where, "Let's agree to disagree," comes into its own. It's OK for people to disagree or have a different viewpoint – if others respect their right to hold that view. We all have different points of reference in life, based on our experiences, knowledge and upbringing, which is great because it means we have the opportunity to learn from each other. Next time you're in a situation where your perspective differs from someone else's, ask them questions about their opinions and ensure you get a chance to voice your own, by using the assertiveness tips we explored on page 90.

If you feel pressured into agreeing with someone else and it doesn't feel right, you don't have to change your view to suit them. You can respectfully end the conversation any time you like.

Can you think of a time when you've disagreed with a loved one or colleague because of difference of opinion? What happened?

Now think of a time when you changed your mind – what caused you to do that?

Comparison is the thief of joy

Never has a truer word been spoken (courtesy of Theodore Roosevelt). Think about it – if we're constantly evaluating our own lives against the impossible yardstick that we measure everyone else's lives by, then we're destined to be unsatisfied. And who wants to live a life like that?

When we have low self-esteem, we tend to judge ourselves particularly harshly (thanks, inner critic), so it's all too easy for comparison to creep in and steal our joy. Everyone else seems to be succeeding where we've failed or accomplishing amazing feats when we've barely managed to brush our hair that morning. But all it really comes down to is a bit of self-love and compassion. When we're kinder to ourselves, and recognize our own skills and abilities as individuals, we don't need to compare ourselves to others.

We also tend to forget the filter effect. When we're online, it's easy to fall into the trap of comparing your no-filter, messy life with a narrow, curated, filtered version of someone else's. But it's not the whole story – after all, their behind-the-scenes is probably not dissimilar to yours. Even celebrities and influencers (who are real people, remember) have a ton of stuff going on in their lives that they don't want to share with the world, but we only get to see the snapshot they want us to see. We're the ones living with our failures, the embarrassing or boring bits and the hard work that goes into just being a human. It may not be fun and glitzy all the time, but it's an authentic life, and it's yours – warts and all.

The simple message is:

> **Don't compare your behind-the-scenes
> with someone else's highlight reel.**

A fantastic way to foster a positive attitude towards your own life, which will help you stop comparing yourself to others, is to make a list of all the unique skills and abilities that you have to offer. Perhaps you're an absolute legend when it comes to baking a Victoria sponge. Or maybe you're the person everyone wants on their team at the pub quiz. Whatever achievements you're proud of, record them below and reflect on how far you've come.

Life resumé of

_____

Skills (e.g. expert roller-skater)

_____

_____

_____

_____

_____

Personal qualities (e.g. loyal and trustworthy)

_____

_____

_____

_____

_____

Thing I am most proud of...

_____

_____

_____

_____

Thing I will be remembered for in the future...

_____

_____

_____

_____

There's only one you

EACH HUMAN BEING IS UNIQUE, UNPRECEDENTED, UNREPEATABLE.
René Dubos

When we have low self-esteem, it's easy to fall into the trap of overthinking what makes us different from those around us. Instead of embracing our individuality, we blame it for making us stand out, or we convince ourselves that what makes us unique is a flaw or a weakness.

Yet being unique is our biggest asset in life. Our emotions, personality, tastes, appearance – everything about us is a one-off blend, never to be repeated. When you think about it like that, it's a little bit mind-blowing! Just like everybody else, you are utterly irreplaceable, complex, and worthy of respect and joy. And that's definitely something to celebrate.

The value of having values

Values are the qualities and beliefs that are important to you. Values give our lives meaning, and in many cases help us to feel genuinely happy and fulfilled. Everyone has different values, but one thing psychologists agree on is that incorporating a set of values into your daily life helps your "feel good" factor reach its highest potential.

Perhaps you prize honesty more highly than kindness and wouldn't hesitate to tell a friend when their outfit doesn't suit them. Conversely, perhaps your friend values kindness over honesty, and if the situation were reversed, would tell you a harmless lie about your outfit choice to make you feel better about it. Neither is wrong, although it has the potential to provoke a minor disagreement! But what's important is that both people are acting within their own value system and being true to themselves.

When it comes to values, your negative thoughts are your friends. If they're bringing you down, you can use them as a signpost to the areas in your life where you need to focus your values. If you feel that life is a bit bleurgh and dreary, then perhaps you're not honouring your value of passion or excitement, and need to build this into your life more. Or if you're struggling to achieve your goals and your mind is telling you that you're inadequate, then fostering determination will help.

What are the core values that guide your life? Turn the page to discover what yours might be.

My core values

Tick the box to indicate how important each of these values is to you:

	Very important	Quite important	Not important
Loyalty			
Creativity			
Honesty			
Kindness			
Optimism			
Passion			
Empathy			
Cheerfulness			
Reliability			
Positivity			
Realism			
Seriousness			
Humour			
Discipline			
Health			
Control			
Spirituality			
Helpfulness			
Knowledge			
Ethics			

This list is by no means exhaustive! Take a moment to think about the values you live by, some of which may be listed here. If you had to a select your top three, which ones would you choose?

Who do you admire?

If you're struggling to work out which values you consider important, think about who you admire most in life for their character (rather than their skills or achievements). What values do they embody? It doesn't have to be someone in the public eye – it could be a person you look up to in your family, at work or in your friendship group.

I admire _____ **because they have the following qualities:**

E.g. Altruism – they dedicate time to their favourite charity

Integrity – they treat everyone around them as an equal

_____

_____

_____

_____

PART 6

Love your body

How we feel about ourselves physically can have a massive impact on our self-esteem. A 2019 survey, conducted in the UK by the Mental Health Foundation and YouGov, reported that one in five adults (20 per cent) felt shame because of their body image; just over one third (34 per cent) felt down or low about their body; and 19 per cent felt disgusted with their appearance. That's an awful lot of negativity – and not much love for our bodies. Think about it – when was the last time you stood in front of a mirror and said, "I love my beautiful body – every little bit, from the top of my head to the soles of my feet"?

If you spend a lot of time worrying about how you look and feeling ashamed of your body image, it can be hard to cultivate love for it. So, how do we change this? Be kinder to yourself and remember that thoughts are simply thoughts – they aren't facts. The essence of who you are comes from inside you, not from how you look on the outside.

In this chapter, we'll explore ways you can increase your self-love and take care of every beautiful part of yourself (yes, even the soles of your feet).

Self-care + self-love = healthy self-esteem

Research shows that the more we look after our body *and* mind, the more resilient we are when it comes to dealing with life's challenges. We're much better equipped to cope with daily dramas if we've had a good night's sleep, a healthy meal and a good dose of downtime. Sometimes, it really is that simple!

Anything you do for yourself that makes you feel better is self-care. There's no "one size fits all" – what works for one person may be someone else's idea of hell – but what's common to all self-care activities is that you've made a conscious decision to put your needs first. Maybe that's as straightforward as sitting in the garden, drinking a cup of tea and listening to the birds for half an hour, or cranking up your earphones and doing a high-intensity workout. Most importantly, it improves how you feel in your mind and body. If it does, you're almost certainly on the right track.

What's also fab about self-care is that it doesn't have to involve a huge time or financial commitment. In fact, many self-care activities are free. Yippee! Relaxing with an engrossing book – that counts. As does taking a nature walk, having a candlelit bubble bath and watching a film, under a blanket, with the dog. Which self-care ideas work best for you? Jot down some ideas below.

Sometimes, a checklist like this one can really help you stay focused on the self-care basics. Fill in the gaps with your own personal self-care activities and, at the end of the week, you'll have a better idea of where you need to focus your time and energy.

Self-care checklist

	Mon	Tues	Wed	Thurs	Fri	Sat	Sun
Exercise	☐	☐	☐	☐	☐	☐	☐
Drink eight cups of water	☐	☐	☐	☐	☐	☐	☐
Read	☐	☐	☐	☐	☐	☐	☐
Stretch	☐	☐	☐	☐	☐	☐	☐
Do one hobby	☐	☐	☐	☐	☐	☐	☐
Tidy up	☐	☐	☐	☐	☐	☐	☐
Eat veggies	☐	☐	☐	☐	☐	☐	☐
Eat some fruit	☐	☐	☐	☐	☐	☐	☐
Meditate	☐	☐	☐	☐	☐	☐	☐
Go for a walk	☐	☐	☐	☐	☐	☐	☐
Give yourself a compliment	☐	☐	☐	☐	☐	☐	☐
_____	☐	☐	☐	☐	☐	☐	☐
_____	☐	☐	☐	☐	☐	☐	☐
_____	☐	☐	☐	☐	☐	☐	☐

Grow your self-love

Self-care and self-love go hand in hand. Spending time focusing on your own needs and doing something you know will make you feel better is the ultimate act of self-love. But more than that, it's about connecting with your true, inner self and understanding what you need to feel healthy in your mind and body. If you can nurture a deep and meaningful relationship with yourself in this way and accept who you are – including your flaws – you're more likely to be kinder to yourself, especially when your self-esteem is low.

You can do this by making friends with yourself – mind and body – an idea we've already explored a little on page 114. Show yourself the same love and respect that you'd extend to your loved ones. Likewise, don't neglect the needs of your body, either. It too needs to be treated with love and respect – not just because body-love is important for self-esteem, but because your body keeps you alive, day in, day out. Your body allows you to live your life – in whatever shape or form that takes – so showing it a little appreciation from time to time is important and empowering.

If your body is long overdue a thank you for all the hard work it does, try this body-love gratitude worksheet to show your appreciation.

Your body is so much more than your appearance (or how you think you appear to others). Showing your body some appreciation for all the amazing things it allows you to accomplish (mostly without complaint!) will help to increase your self-love and, as a result, your self-esteem.

Body gratitude worksheet

I would like to thank my _____ for _____

_____

I would like to thank my _____ for _____

_____

I would like to thank my _____ for _____

_____

I would like to thank my _____ for _____

_____

I would like to thank my _____ for _____

_____

I would like to thank my _____ for _____

_____

I would like to thank my _____ for _____

_____

I would like to thank my _____ for _____

_____

Body-love affirmations

As we explored on page 42, affirmations are a useful tool for shifting the way we think about ourselves and our bodies. Use this list to choose a handful of statements that resonate for you and repeat them to yourself as often as you can, wherever feels comfortable. Allow yourself to really see them, hear them and feel them, for maximum body-loving effect!

My body deserves love

I get to make decisions about my body

My weight may fluctuate, my value does not

My body takes good care of me

I can take good care of my body

Others' opinions of my body do not affect or involve me

I don't want to look like anyone but myself

Food doesn't have to be the enemy; it fuels and nurtures me

A "perfect" body is one that's keeping me alive

I choose health and healing over diets and punishing myself

My body is awesome; it does awesome things

If I am healthy, I am blessed

Now it's your turn. Writing some of your own body-love affirmations will give you the opportunity to create statements that are personal to you – and personal statements will have the most impact. Use the space below to jot some down.

Pay yourself a compliment

Pick a part of your body that you like (or, if you're having a bad day, that you can tolerate!). It can be anywhere and it doesn't have to be something obvious – perhaps you like the curve of your back, or you have really great definition in your arms. Maybe you want to compliment your stretch marks, because they remind you that beautiful bodies come in all shapes and sizes, or that your body was amazing enough to grow another human. Or perhaps you love the scar on your right leg that reminds you of a life full of adventure.

Can you think of three compliments to pay this part of your body? The compliments could be about how it looks, how it helps you to do something, or even the memories it has helped you create. Talk to yourself as if you were talking to a friend or loved one. Here's an example:

"Your eyes are a beautiful shape. The colour of your irises is so unusual – green-blue with orange flecks. They are totally unique and fit your face perfectly."

Healthy body, happy mood

Exercise and being active isn't just good for your body – it's brilliant for your mind, too. That's because when you exercise, your body releases endorphins – the feel-good chemicals that boost your energy levels – which help you to get into a positive mindset, and reduce pain, stress and anxious thoughts. This is great news for your brain, because it means that if you exercise regularly, it could make a noticeable difference to your self-esteem. And it doesn't have to mean running marathons either. (Phew!) The act of simply moving will help to release tension from your body and calm your emotions. You could go for a gentle stroll, do some weeding in the garden or even some chair-based exercises.

A little exercise and movement built into your daily routine could become part of your healthy self-esteem toolbox and, if you're regularly active, it'll be helping to form a healthy habit too. Here are some of the best forms of exercise for self-esteem, as recommended by experts:

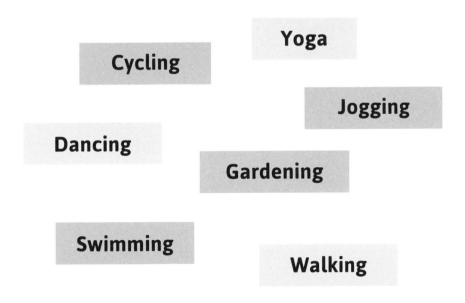

Yoga

Cycling

Jogging

Dancing

Gardening

Swimming

Walking

Exercise planner

Where can you fit exercise into your weekly schedule? Can you find time for a daily activity? Just half an hour every day is enough to have a positive impact on your self-esteem – and if you can keep it up for seven days, you'll be fulfilling the recommended physical activity guidelines set by the World Health Organization. Hurrah!

Fill the planner with your average weekly activities and then see where you can fit some exercise in:

Monday	
Tuesday	
Wednesday	
Thursday	
Friday	
Saturday	
Sunday	

Exercise tracker

Now you know where you can fit your exercise in, use the tracker below to record which activities you've done and for how long. You can also write a few lines underneath each activity to describe how it made you feel – hopefully exhilarated, rather than exhausted!

After a week, you'll be able to get an instant self-esteem boost by looking back and seeing how hard you've worked. It'll also motivate you to keep going! Don't forget to keep hydrated – tick off every glass of water to make sure you're drinking enough – and include a goal for the week, such as walking 10,000 steps a day or yoga three times a week, to give you something to work towards.

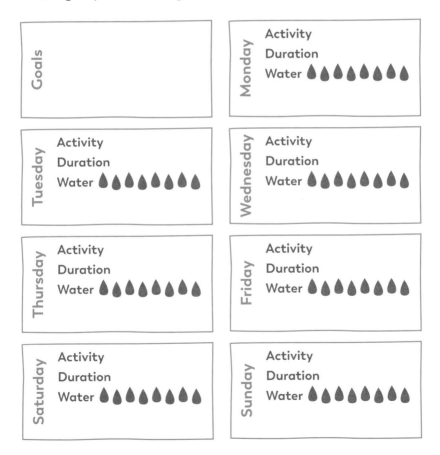

Goals

Monday
Activity
Duration
Water

Tuesday
Activity
Duration
Water

Wednesday
Activity
Duration
Water

Thursday
Activity
Duration
Water

Friday
Activity
Duration
Water

Saturday
Activity
Duration
Water

Sunday
Activity
Duration
Water

Eat well to stay well

Our bodies need fuel to keep them going, and the best way to get fuelled up is to make sure you're eating a nutritious, well-balanced diet. We should all eat a wide variety of foods to ensure we're giving our bodies the best chance to stay healthy and, as we've already discovered, a healthy body equals a healthy mind. According to the World Health Organization, a healthy diet for adults contains protein, fruit, vegetables, legumes (such as lentils and beans), nuts and whole grains (such as unprocessed maize, millet, oats, wheat and brown rice), as well as a little sugar, fat and carbs.

Aim for three meals with healthy snacks in-between. Snacks that are high in vitamins and release energy slowly will help you avoid a drop in your blood glucose, which could make you feel irritable and anxious. When your blood sugar is low, your body releases hormones to keep you going. These hormones have a powerful effect on your emotions (hence the term *hangry*), making you more susceptible to low mood and negativity.

Fight *hanger* with these slow-release snacks:

- Probiotic yoghurt
- Berries
- Almonds
- Guacamole
- Wholewheat crackers
- Toast with peanut butter and sliced banana

Food tracker

Use the tracker to make sure you're fuelling your body with all the nutritional goodness it needs. Aim to tick all five fruit and vegetables by the end of the day – and don't forget that all-important water too, to aid digestion and hydration.

Week of:	Breakfast	Lunch	Dinner	Snacks	Total Calories	Fruit and Veggies	Water
Monday							
Tuesday							
Wednesday							
Thursday							
Friday							
Saturday							
Sunday							

Meal planner

There are lots of recognized benefits to planning meals in advance. You're more likely to reach your health goals, because planning in advance gives you the opportunity to get all the ingredients together before you need to cook, so you're less likely to grab a ready meal or quick but unhealthy option. It also means you can incorporate more variety into your diet, and you won't have the stress of having to plan and prepare a meal at short notice. And don't forget you'll save a ton of money, too! Alongside your meals, you can use the planner to record a daily diet goal, such as "drink less coffee," or "eat an extra piece of fruit."

Monday

Goals

Tuesday

Goals

Wednesday

Goals

Thursday

Goals

Friday

Goals

Saturday

Goals

Sunday

Goals

The power of sleep

A good night's sleep really can make all the difference. Research shows that an optimistic outlook and high self-esteem are closely related to having a beneficial night's sleep – and who hasn't felt highly irritable after a bad night? Most of us! The better you sleep, the more in control of your emotions you are, which means you're less likely to be in the negative frame of mind that low self-esteem thrives on. Additionally, a decent night's sleep aids concentration and gives your body the chance to recover from the stresses of the day. This is also true for your brain – sleeping gives your mind the opportunity to process all the stimuli you have taken in while awake, triggering changes in the brain that strengthen neural connections and help to form memories.

Adults need seven to eight hours' sleep a night – easy for some, wishful thinking for others! The good news is that, for many of us, it may simply be a case of making small lifestyle or attitude adjustments. A useful place to start is by thinking about your night-time routine, which we'll be exploring on the next page.

Night-night, sleep tight

A beneficial night-time routine is crucial to getting those all-important eight hours of shut-eye. Preparing your body and mind for bed by establishing a routine will help you to relax, which means you'll fall asleep more quickly. A healthy bedtime routine looks a little like this:

- **Switch off all screens at least an hour before you turn in – the blue-tinged light can disrupt your circadian rhythm.**
- **Do something enjoyable and relaxing, like taking a bath, writing in a journal or diary, or reading a chapter of a book.**
- **Have a warming drink, such as chamomile tea or hot milk with cinnamon.**
- **Spritz your pillow with some lavender pillow spray and turn down the lights.**
- **Once your head has hit the pillow, listen to a guided meditation or some calming music/white noise.**

It's less about the activity and more about forming relaxing habits, so your body will notice the signals that it's time to wind down and rest.

What's your night-time routine? Create a plan for your ideal routine and include the time you'll undertake each step in the process.

Sleep tracker

Try recording how well you're sleeping on the tracker and consider this in the context of your day. For instance, did you sleep better on the days you got some fresh air and/or exercise? Was your slumber worse when you knew you had to go to work the next day? Considering your sleep patterns in conjunction with your daytime activities helps to form a more complete picture, which makes it easier to spot where you need to adjust your habits.

Today's Date	Time I went to bed last night	Time I woke up this morning	How long I took to fall asleep last night	Total amount of sleep last night	How did I feel this morning? 1 - Wide awake 2 - Awake but a little tired 3 - Sleepy	What I did yesterday

Complete in the morning

PART 7

Friendships and relationships

Research has firmly established the link between healthy self-esteem and healthy relationships. Self-esteem not only affects our view of ourselves, but also how much love we're able to receive and how we connect with others, especially our friends and loved ones.

Our relationship with ourselves provides a template for our relationships with others. So, it makes sense that if we're unhappy with ourselves, these negative feelings will impact on the happiness of our relationships. In addition, self-esteem determines how we communicate with others; the boundaries we set for ourselves and others; our values in life; and our ability to be intimate. It also affects how much influence – both positive and negative – we have over our loved ones. Research has shown that in an intimate relationship, a partner with healthy self-esteem can positively influence his or her partner's self-esteem. The opposite is also true – if low self-esteem is present in a relationship, it can often lead to a negative outcome.

Since self-esteem really can impact our relationships, it's important we spend some time thinking about how our self-esteem could be affecting those around us, and what a healthy (or unhealthy) relationship looks like for you.

Your relationships

Have a think about the people who are important to you and your relationships with them.

Over the next couple of pages, there are a few questions to help you reflect on your connection to them and how this makes you feel.

Who are you closest to? Write their names here. Can you think of one word to describe each friend or loved one?

What qualities make a good friend or loved one?

If one of your friends or loved ones hurt your feelings, would you feel able to tell them? Why?

In what ways are you similar to your friends or loved ones?

In what ways are you different to your friends or loved ones?

How do you feel when you're with your friends or loved ones?

Building healthy foundations

Healthy relationships are built on a foundation of healthy self-esteem. When we feel good about ourselves, our relationships are more likely to be nurturing, because high self-esteem promotes connection and closeness between friends and loved ones. The bond is strengthened further when both parties have healthy self-esteem; their interactions are more likely to be positive, disagreements don't jeopardize the relationship, and there is mutual respect and affection on both sides. This means the relationship is safe and comfortable enough to reach its full potential.

But often when we have low self-esteem, we attract others with similar levels of self-esteem. This is because we feel more comfortable with people who seem familiar to us. We can empathize with their outlook on life, and often share their values and beliefs – even if they are framed in negative terms. We all seek familiarity, but sometimes staying with what we know keeps us in a perpetual cycle of low self-esteem, which is unhealthy for them *and* you.

If this strikes a chord, don't panic – with a little help and support, it's a fixable situation! Over the next few pages, we'll explore how to spot whether low self-esteem is playing a part in your relationships and how to break the cycle of unfulfilling relationships.

Friend or foe?

Whether it's a romantic partner, friend or even a family member, there are certain things to look for in a person that will help you work out whether they're destined to have a positive or negative impact on your life.

You may not be able to choose your family, but if they're having a harmful impact on your self-esteem, there are steps you can take to limit their influence.

Positive	Negative
Lets you be yourself	Puts you down for who you are
Lets you choose your friends	Controls who you see
Replies to your messages	Ignores or ghosts you
Is considerate of your feelings	Treats you like your feelings don't matter
Is interested in your thoughts, feelings and experiences	Only talks about themselves
Makes you feel safe	Makes you feel anxious or unsafe
Laughs with you	Laughs at you
Acknowledges when they've upset you	Refuses to acknowledge they've upset you
They want to hang out with you	They will drop you for other plans

Damage limitation – when relationships go bad

Low self-esteem can make it difficult for us to notice warning signs in our relationships. If you're in a friendship or relationship where you feel unsafe, uncomfortable or unable to leave, it's not your fault and you're certainly not alone. This situation can happen to anyone, and the blame lies solely with the person who is treating you disrespectfully. They may use manipulation, guilt or threats to stop you from walking away, or make you feel worthless, so you don't have the confidence to end the relationship.

There are people you can talk to if you're unsure about someone in your life. Think of a trusted friend or family member you feel comfortable talking to. Then check out page 155 for more resources. Remember – you deserve to be treated with consideration.

- **Take the risk of losing the relationship – if you've expressed how they are making you feel and they don't value you enough to change, you'll have lost nothing by walking away.**

- **Do not tolerate abuse of any kind – create boundaries that you stick to (see next page). For instance, "If you make a comment about my body one more time, I'm leaving." Be prepared to have your boundary tested and make sure you follow it through.**

- **Realize that having a friend or partner is not always better than having no friends or no partner – the best friend you have is yourself. If you're there for yourself, you're never alone.**

Setting boundaries

When we have low self-esteem, it's easy to fall into a trap of people-pleasing. We struggle to communicate what we want and need in a relationship, because we fear how the other person will react. Setting boundaries in our relationships can help us to establish a sense of self-worth and self-respect, which is vital for healthy self-esteem. It also strengthens the connection we have with the other person. While every relationship needs boundaries, they really come into their own in romantic relationships.

One of the hardest boundaries to set in any relationship is the one where we need to express our right to say "no." If we have low self-esteem, we might be reluctant to state how we really feel about something, because we don't want to upset the other person or let them down. The problem is, saying "yes" to everyone's requests can lead us to neglect our own needs. It could be as simple as turning down an invitation or request for a favour from a friend, or to an unreasonable demand by someone who has a negative impact on our self-esteem. Saying "no" is a vital part of self-love and ensures our own needs are being met.

Saying "no" the right way:

● **Be firm and straightforward – you don't need to go into a long explanation. If using the word "no" is uncomfortable for you, you can just say, "That doesn't work for me," instead.**

● **Take your time with the decision – this allows you to assess whether the request fits your own agenda and needs. Ask for more time if necessary.**

● **Establish personal boundaries in all your relationships – if you know your own boundaries, it's easier to navigate the situation when you do need to say "no." Set your boundaries early and make sure the other person is aware of them, too – then everyone knows where they stand.**

Think of a scenario from your own life when you wished you'd said "no" to something, but you ended up doing it anyway. How did that make you feel? Describe the situation below, including any emotions you felt at the time:

If you could go back to that scenario, what would you now say or do instead? Think of ways you might phrase the word "no" that feel comfortable for you to deliver. Jot them down and try to use them next time you're asked to do something you're uneasy with, or you receive an unreasonable request. For instance, "Unfortunately I can't," or "I'll have to pass on that."

Remember, any relationship that requires communication and respect on both sides needs boundaries, and those that have them will be fundamentally stronger than those without.

PART 8

Looking forward

Sometimes it can be scary to look to the future. Unless a clever person creates a crystal ball that's going to tell us exactly what is in store for us – and when – taking a step into the unknown is something we all live with daily. But this experience also presents us with a fantastic opportunity to shape our own lives. Perhaps you're a happy-go-lucky sort of person who likes to leave things to fate. That's perfectly fine and wonderful – but for many of us, setting ourselves goals and planning our journey through life can be a useful way to maintain a positive mindset and keep our mental health on track. Unexpected events will, of course, happen – that's reality. But if we're armed with a plan and a set of tools to manage our self-esteem, the challenges that life throws at us won't seem quite so daunting.

Having healthy self-esteem and maintaining it is a lifelong project – there's no quick fix (unfortunately!). But with the right support and a little self-help, you'll have fewer days feeling bad about yourself and more days knowing you are amazing – and you are enough.

You're not alone

I used to be friends with a group of colleagues who teased me all the time. It made me feel humiliated and annoyed, but they always said they were just joking. When I said I didn't want to spend time with them any more, it made life at work difficult. It took a while to form new friendships and it was hard because my confidence had been knocked, but I have a great group of mates now who care about my wellbeing and respect me, so it was worth it.

Femi, 33

If I see something on social media or online that makes me feel like I need to change my body, I just unfollow. Life's too short to compare myself to strangers on the internet – I'm fabulous exactly as I am.

Alex, 18

I've always been quiet and bookish. Give me a comfy chair, a cup of tea and absolute solitude any day! I used to think there was something wrong with me – that I was boring, and that I should be more outspoken and self-assured. Recently I've learned to accept that being an introvert is a wonderful part of who I am and there's nothing wrong with it.

Jackie, 44

I've always preferred women to men, but growing up I felt like I could never really be me. It was only after I left home that I was able to live the life I wanted without fear of being judged. I'm now living an authentic life where I'm true to myself and I'm so much happier as a result.

Samira, 25

Self-esteem action plan

Creating a plan of action to build and maintain your self-esteem is like future-proofing your mental health. The great news is that by picking up this book, you're already well on the way to improving how you think about yourself. The next step is to craft a solid action plan to make sure you can implement all the things you've learned.

To create your self-esteem action plan, you'll need to consider the following:

- **What life you desire – your goals need to reflect the life journey you're on and where you're headed. Defining your personal vision of success is part of having a healthy self-esteem.**

- **What milestones will you use to track your progress? Once you know what you're aiming for, you can create some mini goals to track your progress. These could be related to some of the self-esteem tips we've talked about – such as learning a new skill or forming new habits.**

- **How you can play to your strengths, as well as supporting your weaknesses. Because we all have different talents and experiences to draw on, your uniqueness will determine how you reach your goal. Even if you have the same goal as someone else, no two paths to reach it are ever the same.**

Time to get planning! Self-esteem affects everyone differently and only you know your current situation, but there are some things we can do to make goal setting that bit easier. Like the "Miracle Question" technique.

If someone promised you that when you wake up tomorrow, you will no longer have low self-esteem, but will feel completely at ease with yourself and confident of your worth, how would you recognise that this had happened? What changes would you notice in yourself that would make it clear that the promise had been kept?

Use the space below to jot down some notes and try to come up with five things that would be immediately different for you. The answers will give you clues to your goals, which we'll be using in the next few pages of the book. For example, perhaps one of the differences you'd see in yourself would be, "I'd be able to walk into a café or bar on my own and strike up a conversation with a stranger," or, "My boss would give me public recognition of my contribution to the department."

Creating goals for the future

Experts agree that having a goal is a fantastic motivator. While every goal is different, they all have something in common – they need a strategy to help you achieve them. Your goal might be related to your self-esteem, or it could be something you want to accomplish. Or perhaps it's a combination of both!

Taking your answers to the Miracle Question on the previous page, use the tracker to write your future goals and then break them down into manageable steps. These might include some of the tips and advice we've already discussed.

Here's an example to get you started. If your answer to the Miracle Question was, "I'd be able to walk into a café or bar on my own and strike up a conversation with a stranger," then your personal goals might be either of the following:

- **I would like to find it easier to socialize with people I don't know.**
- **I would like to have more self-confidence in unfamiliar situations.**

Next, break this down into manageable, actionable steps using the tips in this book. For instance, to achieve more confidence socializing with people you don't know that well, you might need to work on how you feel about yourself first to raise your self-esteem. You could try some of the self-care and self-love tips we've suggested in Part 5, or the self-esteem boosters in Part 2.

Now, you try!

Date: 17/6/2022

Goal:

I would like to feel better about my body image.

Steps:

☐ Use daily positive body image affirmations.

☐ Limit my time on social media

☐ Compliment and thank my body for everything it does

Date:

Goal:

Steps:

☐

☐

☐

Date:

Goal:

Steps:

☐

☐

☐

Ask for help

If you're struggling with low self-esteem, or any other aspect of mental health, there are lots of organizations out there that can provide help and advice. If you feel like your mental health is becoming more than you can manage, it's a good idea to talk with a friend or loved one you trust, and make an appointment with a doctor or healthcare professional.

Anxiety & Depression Association of America

adaa.org

A not-for-profit organization that aims to improve the quality of life for those with anxiety, low self-esteem, depression and other related disorders. Their website includes useful information about mental health and a "find a therapist" directory.

Anxiety UK

03444 775 774 (helpline)
07537 416 905 (text)
www.anxietyuk.org.uk

Advice and support for people living with anxiety, which can be closely linked to self-esteem.

Campaign Against Living Miserably (CALM)

0800 58 58 58
www.thecalmzone.net

Provides listening services, information and support, including a web chat for anyone who needs to talk.

Mind

0300 123 3393

www.mind.org.uk

Includes comprehensive information and support pages, as well as tips for living with anxiety, low self-esteem, depression and other mental health conditions. The website also includes an online community and a crisis resources page with self-help advice to help you cope.

Mental Health America

mhanational.org

Text "MHA" to 741741 to connect with a trained crisis counsellor. Practical advice and support for all aspects of mental health, including links to online communities and tools for long-term wellness.

National Domestic Violence Hotline (US)

1.800.799.SAFE (7233) or text "START" to 88788

www.thehotline.org

Call for free, confidential and compassionate support, crisis intervention information, education and referral services.

Refuge

0808 200 0247

www.refuge.org.uk

Advice about domestic abuse and support for those affected by it.

The National Association for People Abused in Childhood (NAPAC)

0808 801 0331 / support@napac.org.uk

napac.org.uk

A traumatic upbringing or start to life can have a profound impact on self-esteem. NAPAC supports adult survivors of any form of childhood abuse. Offers a helpline, email support and local services.

Conclusion

Congratulations! You've taken your first steps towards healthy self-esteem, and hopefully you're beginning to see a difference in both yourself and your mindset.

Building up your self-esteem and maintaining it will never be easy. It requires patience, dedication and a fair amount of resilience, but making a few simple and effective changes, like the ones we've discussed in this book, will help make the journey that bit easier.

The most important thing is to go at your own pace, knowing that you can come back to this book at any time. It's also OK to make mistakes – you are strong and you can overcome them. It's the mistakes we make that help us to learn and become braver. If you need to, you can always stand still for a moment, pause to take a breath and try again another day.

Remember, you are never alone – you can reach out for help and people will be there to catch you. Life may be full of ups and downs, but if we can learn how to enjoy the ride, we'll be one step closer to living our best lives. Good luck!

Resources

As well as the organizations detailed on pages 152–153, here are some further sources of inspiration and support that you can refer to during your healthy self-esteem journey.

Websites

BACP (British Association for Counselling and Psychotherapy)

www.bacp.co.uk/about-therapy/what-therapy-can-help-with/self-esteem/

BACP's self-esteem pages explain how CBT therapy can help with self-esteem and how to find a therapist, as well as personal stories.

Positive Psychology (Netherlands)

www.positivepsychology.com/category/the-self/

Insightful articles, research and printable worksheets designed by therapists for working on your self-esteem and self-confidence at home.

Psychology Today (USA)

www.psychologytoday.com
Comprehensive catalogue of self-esteem articles and tips, written by qualified therapists and counsellors.

Healthdirect (Australia)

www.healthdirect.gov.au/self-esteem
Tips and advice for working towards healthy self-esteem.

Podcasts

The Confidence and Self Esteem Podcast with James Blundell
A mixture of stories, motivational talks and practical advice to work on your self-love and self-esteem.

The Overwhelmed Brain with Paul Colaianni
Strengthen your self-worth and self-esteem, and learn to make decisions that are right for you with this well-being podcast.

How to Fail with Elizabeth Day
Elizabeth Day celebrates the things that haven't gone right. Every week, a new interviewee explores what their failures taught them and how they moved on.

Books

Beat Low Self Esteem with CBT (2017),
Christine Wilding and Stephen Palmer

How to Deal with Low Self-Esteem (2015),
Christine Wilding

Self-Esteem: Simple Steps to Build Your Confidence (2014),
Gael Lindenfield

The Overcoming Low Self-Esteem Handbook (2021),
Melanie Fennell

Online forums, support groups and communities

www.mentalhealthforum.net/forum (UK)
Friendly peer-support forum for people experiencing mental health issues.

healthunlocked.com/anxiety-depression-support (USA)
Run by the Anxiety & Depression Association of America, this online community is a safe space for those affected by anxiety and depression.

www.anxietycanada.com/resources/mindshift-cbt (Canada)
Download the app for access to the forum, where you can share stories and learn from others' mutual experiences, in a supportive and safe environment.

Saneforums.org (Australia)
A supportive online community where you can chat with others in similar situations.

www.beyondblue.org.au/get-support/online-forums (Australia)
Online support for those living in Australia to achieve their best possible mental health.

Other titles in the series

The Anxiety Workbook

Practical Tips and Guided
Exercises to Help You
Overcome Anxiety

Anna Barnes

ISBN: 978-1-80007-397-5

The Anxiety Workbook contains practical advice, effective tips and
guided exercises to enable you to recognize and process your
anxiety. Based on trusted techniques and mindfulness exercises,
this guide will allow you to better understand your anxiety and will
provide the tools you need to work through it.